MASONIC HALLS OF ENGLAND

The South

Opposite: *Bristol*.

MASONIC HALLS OF ENGLAND

THE SOUTH

The Revd Neville Barker Cryer

LEWIS MASONIC

IAN ALLAN GROUP

In the same series

Masonic Halls of England—The Midlands

Masonic Halls of England—The North

© 1989
N. B. Cryer

Published by Lewis Masonic
IAN ALLAN REGALIA LTD, Terminal House, Shepperton
who are members of the
IAN ALLAN GROUP

First published in England in 1989

British Library Cataloguing in Publication Data
Cryer, Neville B.
  Masonic halls of England.
  The South
  1. England. Freemasons. Lodgers. Halls
  I. Title
  942
ISBN 0 85318 163 2

Printed in Great Britain by
Latimer Trend & Company Ltd, Plymouth

CONTENTS

FOREWORD

FOR MORE than a century Masonic historians have been concerned in researching the origins and development of the Craft. Little, however, appears to have been done in recording the most publicly visible evidence of our existence: the places where we meet. From my own experience of visiting lodges in England and Wales I know the great wealth of history and variation in style evidenced by the many Halls and Lodge Rooms used by our lodges. The Rev. Neville Barker Cryer is to be congratulated both for bringing this aspect of our history to our attention and for recording it now for those who will follow us in years to come.

M. B. S. Higham
Commander, R.N.
Grand Secretary.

PREFACE

THE WRITING OF this book, like the other volumes in this series, has given the author a great deal of pleasure. It has permitted me to appreciate something of the breadth and depth of English freemasonry at the present time as well as allowing me the delight of seeing the wealth of treasures which we still possess and of meeting some of the dedicated masons who have undertaken to preserve for the future those heirlooms they have received from the past.

It has been a journey of constant surprises as door after door has been opened to reveal the temple interiors and their contents, sometimes in almost the same manner as they were first seen 150 or 100 years ago. It is the joy of that discovery, and the interest aroused in seeing so many items of peculiar fascination for the masonic student that led me to believe that we should produce this and the other volumes.

My first concern therefore has been to record for the present generation and for posterity something of what the Craft has handed down to us from its very beginnings in this land. Many, I believe, will, like myself, be pleasantly surprised by the variety and richness of the different halls which are illustrated here, whether it be the Tudor timbering of Faversham or the Regency elegance of Weymouth, the tiny meeting place of Langport or the extensive suites of Park Street, Bristol. Every location has its own fascination especially when, as I hope I have shown, the building also contains particular treasures that are known nowhere else or only rarely so. I hope that this survey of intriguing Southern halls will raise the spirits of masons at this time and make them quietly proud of the heritage that is theirs.

The second purpose of my writing has been to try and encourage a greater diligence throughout our land in looking at and understanding the possessions in freemasonry that we may have in our own locality. It has been my experience that my visit to a temple or its museum has often renewed interest in its contents for the masons who regularly and normally meet there. Too many of us are not aware of the treasure trove that lies around us and there is all the more danger that if this unconscious indifference is not stemmed there could be examples of the kind of loss of previous pieces of the past such as have already occurred in some centres. If you ask some masons in a place that has a long tradition where are their old tracing boards, chapter banner, globes or pillars the answer is either 'we don't know' or 'Ah! now we do have some stacked somewhere'. Once the items are unearthed and explained, as was an Antients' lodge board used in a cloakroom at Barnstaple, there is a new sense of pride awakened and a determination to look after these heirlooms with more care.

Thirdly, I wanted to encourage masons who travel around the country to go and see some of the halls and their contents that are mentioned here. It has long been a custom for people on their holidays to enter an old parish church or a castle or manor house and wonder at the relics of the past of our nation. Here, for freemasons, is the beginning of a guide for some of our peculiar heritage in English history. I hope sincerely that readers will take this book with them on their journeys and ring up the local Provincial or lodge secretary and ask whether a visit to these halls is possible. It will well repay you to see these halls for yourself.

As I have travelled around this land and responded to the information about interesting halls that has been provided for me I have been only too well aware that I may be overlooking some gems of masonic interest that I ought to have included here. Despite the fact that there will be at least two volumes in series with this one—covering the North of England and the Midlands—I am sure that there will be some who will want to draw my attention to treasures overlooked. With the encouragement of the publisher I invite anyone who would wish to do so to write to me at Shepperton and give me details of their hall and its contents. I am sure that future editions of this volume or others in the series can benefit from being kept as comprehensive as possible. It may even be that we shall find ourselves with enough material for yet another volume in the series. It will be good to know that this book has stimulated such interest in *Masonic Halls of England.*

The Revd Neville Barker Cryer
1988

ACKNOWLEDGEMENTS

No BOOK SUCH as this could possibly have been completed without the help of a large number of collaborators. I shall attempt to name many of these below but it would be impossible to mention the countless Provincial Grand Masters, Provincial Secretaries and their staffs who have assisted me with suggestions, contacts, directions for travel, and in some cases actual hospitality. I am deeply grateful to them all and I want to state here that had it not been for them and their work then this book would not even have been possible, and certainly not in the time available.

Having been put in touch with individual halls and the lodges associated with them I specially want to thank the following for their interest before, during and following my visits and for being willing in each case to check the script of my chapters for their hall so that it is as accurate as possible. Any remaining errors must still be laid at my door.

(Barnstaple) L. J. Canham; (Bath) A. E. Gayner; (Bradford-on-Avon) T. G. Golden; (Brighton) J. E. Meaney; (Bristol) R. W. M. Howes; (Canterbury) F. C. Hammersley; (Cheltenham) P. M. Dyke; (Faversham) E. T. Mount; (Jersey) D. G. Perrin and A. C. F. Jackson; (Lewes) R. E. Hawkins; (Langport) W. J. Dagworthy; (Liskeard) R. E. Crabb; (Exeter) J. J. L. Gore; (Newport) J. Barrett and George A. Holden; (Poole) J. R. Longhurst and S. A. H. Swain; (Taunton) R. T. F. Tucker, T. Hughes and R. Walker; (Weymouth) F. J. Cooper; (Windsor) K. A. Brown (deceased). Thanks are also due to John Hamill, librarian and curator of the United Grand Lodge of England library and museum for assisting in the supply of illustrations. To numerous photographers who have supplied illustrations, some anonymously, and to all of these brethren, as well as many others whose names I have not recalled, I extend the very warmest of thanks and express my delight at making so many more masonic friends.

1 Barnstaple
2 Bath
3 Bradford-On-Avon
4 Brighton
5 Bristol
6 Canterbury
7 Cheltenham
8 Exeter
9 Faversham
10 Jersey
11 Langport
12 Lewes
13 Liskeard
14 Newport
15 Poole
16 St Austell
17 Taunton
18 Torbay
19 Weymouth
20 Windsor

10

BARNSTAPLE

A Prize of Trafalgar Vintage

ANYONE APPROACHING BARNSTAPLE from the south will enter the town by crossing the bridge over the River Taw. If the visitor then turns right along the road to the right as if making for South Molton it will shortly lead him to a green space on the right which is bordered by five houses of Regency character with their pillared fronts, large first floor windows and gracious stepped entrances. The name of the area is Trafalgar Lawn and the property at No 4 was built for Lewis Hole, RN, a first lieutenant on the *Revenge* at the Battle of Trafalgar. It was bought from his prize money received for heroic conduct and is distinguished from the neighbouring houses by having its main entrance at the side instead of facing the lawns that rightly gives the place its name. It was here that in 1966 a Dedication Service took place as the local masons sought to make this their future home. WBro the Rev Mr Shelmerdine said appropriately on that occasion, considering the naval origin of the premises and the outpourings at a consecration occasion—'Why the Lodge is decanted from Vessel to Vessel I do not know, but we do know that the consequent wine, a spirit of Freemasonry, is of excellent vintage'. When one considers the prize items contained in this veritable treasure house of a masonic hall today it can only be said that its present function is worthy of the honourable fellow who first procured it.

Before entering the home of Loyal Lodge No 251 and the other Barnstaple masonic units that meet here it will be well if we consider something of the past history of Freemasonry in the borough.

It was in 1762 that the Lodge of the Fleece, No 281, had established itself as one of the 10 masonic lodges then meeting in Devon. Unfortunately it lapsed in 1766 and it was not until 23rd September, 1783 that the Craft was again restored with the granting of a warrant for the Loyal Lodge to meet at the Globe Inn, Cross Street. It is important to realise that in terms of access Barnstaple was virtually unreachable by land at this time and its earliest masonic influences probably came from Ireland, or at least from the Grand Lodge of the Antients. One way in which this happened was by the creation of two lodges associated with the North Devon Militia. The HQ of one Militia lodge was in Ebberley Lawn in the town whilst the other, Good Intention Lodge No 452, was in Bideford where there was much concern about the conflict in the American colonies or the intentions of a 'Hostile France'. Both these military lodges, of course, had a travelling warrant and could, when they encountered the Loyal Lodge members, tell them of their masonic experiences elsewhere. 'The Eight Brothers Lodge No 228' was in fact an Antients lodge and there is a record of its meeting with Loyal Lodge in 1814 to see the reobligation of the latter's members after the Act of Masonic Union and to instruct the loyal brethren in the New Ritual and Practices as well as to introduce the election (*sic*) of 2 Deacons. What may surprise the student of masonry in this area even more is the fact that not until 1809 is there any indication of the third degree being introduced. On August 15th the minutes read as follows:

> Fellow Craft opened in due form
> Lodge of Emergency held—
> Lodge closed in due form—
> At this lodge Night Brother Shadgett
> was promoted from Fellowcraft to
> the Sublime Degree of a Master Mason.

There is also ample evidence of the practice of the ceremony of 'Passing the Chair' to qualify brethren for admission to the Holy Royal Arch even though the first Barnstaple Chapter was in 1821. Antients lodges, it should be remembered, were licensed to practice the 'fourth degree' within their Craft warrants.

Before the Loyal Lodge moved yet again to the Assembly Rooms, Boutport Street in the 1840s the brethren had aquired one of their most treasured possessions and a wonderful ornament for their present Temple. This was the Bath furniture and the precious jewels that came with it.

The manner in which this furniture was acquired forms a remarkable story that begins with the opening in a blaze of glory of a masonic hall in York Street, Bath. This opening was performed by no less a personage than HRH Frederick Augustus, Duke of Sussex, the Grand Master of England, on 23rd September, 1819. Three lodges were to use the hall (see the chapter on Bath in this volume) and soon the Finance Committee had to acknowledge that they could not meet the overheads and mortgage repayments that were involved. A solution had to be found.

This was offered when Bro Charles Geary, a Bath wine merchant and a prominent member of Royal Cumberland Lodge, was prepared to pay off all the debts so that by March 1823 he was the sole proprietor. It was not the end of the story by any means. During the following years there was an increasing trouble about rent arrears and on July 18th, 1842, the hall which had cost £3000 to erect was sold for a mere £1300. Bro Geary then decided to dispose of the hall's furniture in one lot 'by way of chance' in January of 1843. Tickets were sold at 21s each or five for £5. The members of Loyal Lodge, at Barnstaple, decided to invest £10 in the draw.

The Freemasons' Quarterly Review in March 1843 records that the draw took place but that as only 200 shares had been sold Bro Geary withdrew 50 shares for the benefit of the subscribers. The winning number was 212—and this was a number held by Bro Geary. As a result Bro Geary then issued a circular in which he offered the entire lot at a reduced figure of 100 guineas or, if preferred, the whole divided into lesser lots at proportionate sums.

The superb appointments in Barnstaple's Masonic Hall include these impressive pillars and beside the Master's chair can be seen globes mounted on ornate plinths. The Hall, like some others in this book boasts a fine ceiling complete with signs of the Zodiac.

Despite the fact that they had already failed in the draw the Loyal Lodge members made another quick decision. They offered to take the lot, especially as the WMs chair was itself considered to be worth £50! The purchase money was raised by the lodge taking 16 shares of £1 10s each, the Chapter three and 45 individual brethren took 81 shares, which raised a sum to cover also the transport and any other expenses for the acquisition of this furniture. There remained one final difficulty.

The Loyal Lodge was then meeting in a private room at 8 Cross Street where there was enough furniture for all its needs. Now that they had 'the splendid and celebrated Bath masonic furniture and paraphernalia' they decided to remove to the Assembly Rooms. The Quarterly Review again remarked:

> The Bath Masonic Furniture ... has undergone a complete renovation and, being displayed to the greatest advantage in the elegant and capacious ballroom, forms as splendid and perfect a coupe d'oeil as any lodge in England; and more particularly the effect of the newly initiated candidates. . . .

The article continued:

> It is a case of congratulations to the Craft in general, that this splendid furniture which was collected and arranged at Bath regardless of expense, has not now been dispersed, but is again restored to its legitimate purpose, under the guardianship of this lodge. The candlesticks are especially worth notice, as it is said that but three sets were ever cast, one for the Grand Lodge of England, another for the Grand Lodge of Prussia, and the third set in this collection. They are of ormolu, of most elegant and delicate workmanship, with allegorical silver plates inlaid. . . .

It is this truly impressive collection of masonic items that immediately draws one's attention when at last entering the temple at 4 Trafalgar Lawn. The actual date of the chairs is not at all certain but surmounting the back of the W. Master's chair there is a coronet with three large gilded feathers, the Prince of Wales' plume, and since the Prince (afterwards King George IV) was Grand Master from 1790 to 1813 the deduction could well be that it was made about 1800.

Each of the principal chairs has its own very distinctive design. That of the Master, with its gilt spiral legs and curved, carved and scroll-ended arms, has an especially beautiful back. On a black back-ground a centrepiece of pleated yellow silk forms a large circle with a highly decorated gilded rim and an eight-sided star motif at its centre. At the bottom corners are, on the left, a gilded beehive with eight bees about it, and, on the right, a level with an extended pair of compasses above. Immediately over the silken circle are 7 golden stars with a faced sun in full glory and a crescent moon, also with a face, flanking them. Above the stars is a phoenix rising from attendant flames.

The back of the chair is flanked by two gilded and fluted Corinthian columns bearing above their chapiters a globe apiece on small tripods. Between them is a curved headpiece surrounded by scrollwork and, on a black background within, a triangle superimposed on a Glory with a large black eye at its centre. It is this curved headpiece which carries the Prince of Wales plume already referred to. What further enhances the chair is that it is itself flanked by two imposing rococo pedestals on the top of which there are again two antique globes in quadruped stands, themselves so elevated as to be on a level with the headpiece of the chair. Above the chair and on a red curtained panel which hangs from the roof there is a large 16 pointed star with a five pointed and illuminated centrepiece which is used for displaying 'that bright morning star' which is part of the ceremonies here. Moreover the pedestal in front of the chair is itself a lovely work of art being inlaid mahogany showing the symbols of the WM, SW and JW, as well as that of a PM, at the corners and between them a golden circle with a black background, a large G at the heart of a six-pointed star itself on a glory. With the lovely candlestick beside it the whole effect is one of tasteful elegance and rich antiquity.

Passing to the west between two plain white columns on tall square bases, with the large wooden plinth holding the tracing boards covering most of the chequered carpet, we come to two more columns of similar design save that these are made of brass and carry on their heads the brass bowls which are covered with a gilded netting. Between them is a red plush kneeling stool. We thus arrive at the place for the Senior Warden, to find at the foot of his tasteful but undecorated pedestal an ancient replica in white of the two tablets of stone bearing the Roman numerals I to X. (Cf. the similar item at Taunton). Over this item and resting on the floor is a miniature Jacob's ladder forming a centrepiece between the numerals.

With its attendant ormolu candlestick the SW's chair well matches that of the WM for workmanship. Though the decoration is of inlay rather than appliqué the back is of delicately decorated oak between 2 gilt and fluted columns which bear a gilt circular ball. In the centre of the back is a large gilt oval with an oval of swag within and a level, headed by a formally tied ribbon, at its heart. Above the back of the chair is a semicircular headpiece similar to that of the WM with a gilt surround and inside it a triangle enclosing an all-seeing eye and a glory that covers the whole of the space. Above this again and stretching between the balls at the top of the

The back panel of the Master's chair which forms part of the 'Bath' furniture.

pillars is another large decoration—scrollwork in gilt bearing a golden circle with rays and within it a gilt level and ribbon on a dark blue background. The arms and legs are most minutely carved with other masonic emblems all round the base of the seat and tops of the legs.

The third chair, that of the JW, is again quite distinctive. It is set in an alcove in order to to avoid encroachment on the limited space around the tracing boards and above it hangs a five-pointed gilt star with a large G superimposed. The chair itself has less decorated, but still gracefully carved, arms and above the oval brown leather back there is perched a leaning volume sideways on with the imitation ribbed spine of a well-bound book. The frame of the chair is again in the form of two fluted pillars but they are of natural wood and only have their decorative heads and balls gilded.

Beside the JW's chair are two of the junior officers' chairs from an earlier period. They are more modest in design, of painted black wood with a leather studded back and triangular headpieces. One of them bears a deacon's symbol but the other has none. These upright chairs contrast markedly with the two very ample armchairs that flank the dais for the Master. These are fine late eighteenth century pieces which are probably the only items left from the days before the Bath furniture was acquired. The back and seat are plush lined with elegantly carved backs and arms and at the head of the back is an oval panel which shows in the one case the symbol of a PM and in the other an open VSL in a triangle for the Chaplain.

It can well be imagined that these above items alone make this a most memorable building but they are not by any means the total of what can be seen here. Mention has been made of the large container for the tracing boards and these, when laid to view, are again notable. Though not as unusual as some that are elsewhere described in this volume they are individually painted and show, in contrast to many others, no figures on the ladder in the one degree, an especially long staircase in the second degree and a most magnificent entrance porch to the Sanctum Sanctorum in the third degree (not to mention a pair of unusual cyphers).

What also deserves mention is that when the 3° is being performed in the working here the box containing the tracing boards is removed so that the chequered floor can be folded back to reveal a cavity with white walls some four feet deep, and at its base a full sized black wooden coffin containing a winding sheet bearing a real skull and two crossed human bones. The candidate does indeed stand on the very brink of a grave!

Above that cavity recess the roof of the temple is decorated with a most colourful circle of the Zodiac, and hanging from its centre is a large and circular chandelier with a G also pendant beneath. These are reminders of an older masonry that we also see elsewhere in the room and the hall. On entering the temple, for example, there is a most distinctive decoration above the double doors. It is a large representation of a rainbow bearing the gilt letters 'I T N O T G A O T U'. Within the semicircle thus formed is a smaller arc of a halo and this in turn encloses a golden triangle with an open VSL at its centre. One can only assert that this conveys that sense of the true 'Noachidae' which is how Anderson describes freemasons in his earliest Constitutions.

Above the simple folding table, which is currently the cramped place for the Secretary and Treasurer along the north wall, there is a most unusual DIAL. It is

An actual fellowcraft's staircase. Each of the steps bears an initial of the seven liberal arts and sciences.

thought to have come from Bath and it is really a masonic clock (not at present working) in a gold frame, set on a Seal of Solomon (or 2 interlaced triangles). The fascinating thing is that this item, which is about 3 feet across, has at its centre the circle within two parallels and an open VSL at their head with a G beneath. The figures around the black dial are made up of masonic implements and symbolic items so that 9 o'clock is represented by three pillars, one upright and two crossed (IX) with a sprig of acacia on the outer side. Four o'clock is shown by one upright pillar and up-ended calipers (IV) with a trowel on the outer side, and so forth. The place for the Secretary is shown by a lockable wooden box fixed to the wall with another gilded plume of feathers beneath, two gilded crossed quill pens, and what is obviously a simulated page in metal of a minute book with an entry in the early 1800s.

Three other items of peculiar interest must be noted before we take our leave of this building. The first is the unique winding staircase that formed part of the 'Bath' set and is a charming curved flight of seven treads each of them bearing the initial of one of the 7 liberal arts and sciences. This balustraded stair then fits into a charming 'Middle Chamber' built like a gazebo with a delicate canopy of scalloped wooden panels and slender wood supports. The whole effect is most impressive, especially as it is placed on the upstairs landing against a charming stained glass window, which allows soft light to illuminate the feature.

In the anteroom to the temple below we see the shields that tell us of an early Knight Templar activity in this area, and below them are pictures illustrating the lodge furniture set out in the Castle Street hall and some pictures of the Bath furniture when first received.

As we might come to put on our coats to leave we shall find in the cloakroom beside the elegant entrance hall a glass-topped table with its own pre-Union tracing board. Here is a coloured representation of a board for all the combined degrees—3 candles between 2 pillars, a representation of the 2 tables of the Law, the rough and smooth ashlars, the two parallels with a circle between supporting a ladder leading up to the VSL and a large gilt triangle with an all-seeing eye in a glory. Flanking these upper symbols are, on the left, a tracing board, a pot of incense and the sun at meridian; and on the right, a level, plumbline and square with the flowering rod of Aaron and the moon and seven stars in the heavens. It is a most remarkable thing to be greeted with on arrival and its lodgement in such a lovely closet only goes to show how rich is this lovely meeting-place so that what for some lodges would be a priceless possession is but a fringe item in an outer room.

Truly the visitor to Barnstaple has a feast of good things to see and to appreciate. It is indeed the prize of Trafalgar Lawn.

BATH

One of Bath's Treasures

THE MASONIC HALL in this lovely city stands in Old Orchard Street. Nothing of the original purpose of the area is very visible today though once there was an orchard that extended as far as the river and the site belonged to the Benedictine Priory of which Bath Abbey parish church is the continuing reminder. The actual location of the present hall was outside the old Borough wall and was thus part of property that came to the Duke of Kingston in 1715. It was from him that John Hippisley, a London actor of repute, sought to acquire the site for a theatre in Orchard Street. Hippisley belonged to a well known West Country family and was a member of the popular freemasons' lodge that met at St Paul's Head Tavern in Ludgate Street, London. It was hardly suprising that he met with some success in trying to raise the necessary funds from people like Beau Nash and Quin, another actor and fellow mason. One other contributor, John Palmer, took over the project when Hippisley died and it was he that planned the success that attended the stage plays in this building from October 1750. By 1786, after much effort, the Bath theatre obtained the title and patent of Theatre Royal. It continued to flourish until July 13th, 1805.

These premises stood unused for four years and then in 1809 the Roman Catholic authorities of Prior Park and Downside acquired it for conversion into a church and provided an organ, the present dais, columns and an underground passage to the nearby priest's house. The galleries and stage were mostly dismantled but the gallery at the west end, now turned into a very pleasant upper dining room, and the distinctive small chapel behind the reredos, were developed. The Catholics used it until 1858.

It was in 1866 that it was finally acquired by the freemasons and on December 3rd Lodges 41, 53 and 379 began to make regular use of the building. Reminding even present day masons of the past of this unusual temple there is, on the left as you face the reredos, the remains of a Stage box whilst behind the reredos you can still see the stairs that led to a similar box that was removed to accommodate the organ. This instrument, impressive at least in its design and appearance, was formerly in the chapel of Bath College which no longer exists.

The pictures on the reredos are by Barker, the well known Bath artist, and are intended to be representations of King Solomon, Hiram of Tyre and Hiram Abiff. Their size and colour form a very distinctive backcloth for any ceremony. At the other end of the temple you will see a huge wall canvas that depicts Christ and the lame man at the pool of Bethesda. It was painted by William Hoare in 1768 and came from the Octagon Chapel in Milsom Street. It was presented to the freemasons of Bath in those days and shows a somewhat healthier relationship between chapel and Craft.

All around the walls is the warm oak panelling that came from the pews that were used in the Roman Catholic chapel. These not only create a richer backcloth for the other seating but also provide useful storerooms on the north and south sides of the temple. They are also the surface for a series of colourful coats of arms which are all explained in an illustrated MS register that is kept in the museum. The whole effect, especially with the furniture to which I shall shortly refer, is of a spacious, lofty, distinctive and colourful arena for what is a different masonic ritual in many repects. For the masonic drama an ex-theatre and church seem just right. It should also be said that the ante-room is no less impressive.

As we look at the contents of this historic site today we need to remember that it once contained the beautiful masonic furniture which was sold to, and which now adorns, the Masonic Hall at Barnstaple—another subject of this volume. That sale took place in 1843 and the three lodges which surrendered these items were the Royal Cumberland, the Royal York Lodge of Perfect Friendship and the Lodge of

The pillars with netting are some of the finest to be seen in the South of England. The reredos in the east is equally impressive. Note the shields around the walls.

The 'restored' Bath Master's chair.

Virtue. The Royal Cumberland Lodge is certainly aware of what a loss it was that their predecessors effected. However, there is on the dais in the main Temple an outstanding piece of masonic furniture—the Master's Chair. It is generally assumed that this is a perfect replica of the original Royal Cumberland item which Charles Geary sold to the Loyal Lodge at Barnstaple. The present chair was presented by the late WBro A. Leonard Fuller together with the oak platform that supports it. The chair was made by the prominent Bath firm of Mallet and Son. WBro Bruce Oliver (writing about this Bath furniture in *Ars Quatuor Coronatorum* Vol 57 of 1944), gives his opinion that it is modelled on the original Master's chair for the Lodge of Virtue whilst the Master's chair from the Royal Cumberland is now the one used by the Senior Warden in Barnstaple. They are all excellent and fascinating examples of the masonic decorator's art and provide much visual encouragement for that 'daily advancement in masonic knowledge'.

It should not be imagined that this one delightful piece is the only major item of interest. Far from it. The Royal Cumberland Lodge held their first meeting here on 6 December, 1866, three days after the hall had been consecrated for masonic use. This lodge was so perturbed at the loss it had sustained that it made most determined efforts to more than replace the furniture it once had.

One chair seems to have escaped disposal and it is the one occupied by the Director of Ceremonies who sits, it should be noted, in the centre of the *north* side of the lodge flanked by the lodge stewards whose red aprons (in an ordinary Craft and not Grand or Provincial Grand Lodge) are yet another striking difference in this the second oldest Provincial private lodge in England. The DC's chair bears on its back a brass plate on which is engraved, 'Presented to the Royal

The large ancient tracing boards. Of particular interest is the third board (right) with unusual masonic symbols illustrated not used today

Cumberland Lodge No 48 Friday May 16th, 1834 By Brother John Johnson, PMSW.'

The pedestals at present in situ are also worth noting. The main one, placed before the Master's personal one, was provided in 1883 when Royal Cumberland were celebrating the 150th anniversary. It is a most attractive item, just as are the two oak carved chairs on the dais, the Glastonbury chair used by the Inner Guard, and the unusual Oak ballot box kept under the DC's pedestal—yes, even he has one!

Most striking of all the Cumberland furniture, however, is the ancient third degree tracing board which stands out even amongst the other old boards that this lodge and the temple's other lodges possess. This particular board has a wealth of pre-Union symbols (that is, before 1813) and the remarkable thing is that it is still explained in full as part of the normal lodge ritual. It is so large that it needs two men at least to manhandle it into position onto the floor of the lodge, though supported by a stand, and its being so placed makes abundantly clear why there was from those early days the need to square the lodge when it was opened. Anyone who can have the opportunity to hear that lecture on the tracing board will be amply rewarded with a masonic blessing in instruction. They will also learn in a craft setting about the Ark of Noah, the Pot of Manna and the Hour-glass.

Mention must be made of the Lodge of Honour tracing boards that are here illustrated. It is a matter of deep regret for the lodge that the set is not now complete for the third degree one disappeared some years ago. The two that remain were painted by Arthur Loutherburgh Thiselton who had, during his youth, been a scene painter in Drury Lane theatre. They have both been well described by WBro Haunch in 1963 and WBro Saunders in 1975. They came into the possession of the Lodge in 1825 and are very much treasured today.

Nothing so strikes the attention of the visitor from the London area as the two great pillars that stand alongside the wide kneeling stool in the middle of the large floor but just forward of the Senior Warden's chair and pedestal. We shall see pillars in many parts of the lodge rooms that we visit but here they stand out in the wide expanse of this temple and certainly remind every candidate and member of the porchway or entrance to King Solomon's Temple. One can hardly deny that they add materially to the general dignity and splendour of this hall as already suggested.

Before leaving the temple one must make a detour behind the great reredos and see the tiny chapel which is used in the Knight Templar ceremony at Bath—a ceremony that again has many old and distinctive features. The chapel is intimate and is a church in miniature with a chancel or sanctuary and a small nave. Only a very limited number can be present at any one time but experience has shown me that the use of this unique spot adds materially to the impressiveness of the ceremonial carried out there.

Mention of the Knights Templar order leads to a few more details about the coats of arms which were mentioned briefly above. The use of shields like this on the walls of what was a Knights Templar encampment or Preceptory is echoed in our visits to Exeter, Cheltenham and even Weymouth. Soon after the foundation of the Bladud Preceptory No 40 it was agreed that as the Founders and early Eminent Preceptors were all entitled to bear their own arms they should emblazon shields with their own coats rather then employ the pseudo-heraldry then in use.

The large shields now visible are the remainders of those and only seven have survived. About the year 1890 it has to be assumed that the need for space led to smaller shields being encouraged and these were probably executed for the knights by one of the coach-painters in the firm of Messrs Fuller of Bath. Their presence serves to remind the Craft masons of other branches of Freemasonry all around them.

To have seen and enjoyed this hall so far is not to have in any way exhausted its treasures. The ante-room with its magnificent Honours Boards, which occupy all the walls and are so exquisitely designed and decorated, is a fitting introduction to the main meeting place and this is further added to by the large terrestrial Globe which is kept on the staircase platform. There were once two such globes which presumably added yet again to the dignity of the lodge room (as we see elsewhere) and a picture of 1933 shows them *in situ*.

Moving up the staircase we find not only a most tasteful dining room but also, at the top of the house, a well appointed museum in which there are so many items of yet further interest. One item must suffice to stir interest. It is a Third Degree Star. In 1856 Bro Charles Hasler, who repainted the Cumberland tracing boards, was requested to 'have a lantern erected which he had invented, and considered would be a great improvement to the lodge, especially in the third degree'. It is a most ingenious production—as is also the later one designed to be lit up by gas!

Here then is a Masonic Hall of real antiquity, not built as such but now admirably suited to its purpose. It is a hall that properly fits into the great City it serves. It is one of Bath's and masonry's treasures.

BRADFORD-ON-AVON

A Wool Clothier's Heritage

BETWEEN 1538 AND 1540 the Tudor antiquary and librarian to Henry VIII, John Leland, visited the already ancient wool town of Bradford-on-Avon. In his famous work, the Itinerary, he speaks of a rich clothier named Horton who had died but a short time before though his widow was still alive. This merchant lived, writes Leland, in a house built by himself 'at the north est part by the Chirch' (*sic*). He also built: 'a goodly large chirch house "ex lapide quadrato" at the est end of the chirch yard without it.' This latter building is still standing and is situated in Church Street. Some have suggested that the building was for purely parish business but it seems more likely to have been used as the Guild Hall of the woollen industry in Bradford.

About 1629 it was being let to a tenant at a rate of £3.00 per annum and we know from those same records that the house then measured 73 ft by 23 ft. By about 1660 the Lord of the capital manor had let part of it to a George Reynolds for £1 15s, and subsequently some of the building was turned into cottages. What is clear is that the building marked on a map of 1743 was the place in which, before the days of rating as we know it, meetings were held for raising funds for church repairs, caring for the poor and other local necessities.

From 1873 to 1903 it became the Free School, which was transferred there from the Saxon Church a short distance away, and it was when this purpose was no longer required that in 1912 the Town Hall Co. offered the accommodation to the Lodge of Friendship and Unity, No 1271, who are the current lessees. The first rent was for £12 a year and the lodge members were to put the building into a state of good repair. They readily responded and the essential improvements were made. Later, the premises were purchased by a WBro Wallington who most generously bequeathed them to Holy Trinity Church and the lodge jointly, with the temple and adjoining rooms left to the lodge in 1922 under a lease for 999 years! In 1922/3 the whole building was restored in its original style under the direction of WBro Breakspeare, an architect of local repute. The resultant work is most impressive. One cannot wonder at the lodge being justly proud of their distinctive home. Certainly it is a hall that fits naturally into the attractive Cotswold style of the rest of the town.

Entering through what appears to be a doorway of one of the eighteenth century cottages and beneath a wrought iron lantern, that proudly displays the square and compasses to all the passers-by, you enter a small vestibule. The door to the left leads into a spacious room used for Church Council matters amongst which is a Day Club run by parish volunteers for providing refreshments to senior citizens of the town. The room has one fascinating feature from the past. This is a mullion window at ground level and on the west wall of the house. It is protected on the outside by a wrought iron spike that projects from the sill up to about half the window's height. This window is in the form of an arrow slit measuring 8 in wide on the outside and 34 in within. It is said that this was the window through which dues were paid to the poor, following the Poor Laws of the seventeenth century, and later the wages of the cottage weavers of the woollen industry who gathered outside it. The spike was to prevent anyone reaching in to take more than they were entitled to, or fastening a hold on the payer.

Turning from the vestibule through the door to the right one enters a low-ceilinged and oak-panelled room with a fireplace on the inside wall and two mullioned window recesses on the outer one. The rough-hewn beams and close rafters give the room real character and with the mahogany table in the centre and a rich coloured carpet this is an ante-room in which the brethren gather easily before their meetings. It is a room which contains several items of historical interest including glass and crockery, two old aprons in frames on the wall, and on the far wall an illuminated oil painting of the lodge's benefactor. One other item kept in this room is a silver trowel which was presented to the lodge by VWBro F. B. Brook, MA. Grand Treasurer and inscribed '1942—To spread the cement of friendship . . . '. This trowel is still regularly used by the Director of Ceremonies for

The lantern and symbol above the entrance.

indicating the Fire after the Tyler's toast.

At the far end of the room there are two doors. The door to the left leads through the robing room and toilet area to an outside flight of stairs which allows access to the upstairs dining room. This is currently sparse in decoration but readily confirms the antiquity of the property. The uneven floor, the wide, open fireplace and the mullioned windows that match those below, all suggest a less cosseted period of English living. Apart from dining and other masonic functions this room is let to other local users from time to time for varying purposes and there is no intention to alter its original character. The right hand double doors on the ground floor lead into the transverse area that runs at right angles and turns the whole house into a T formation. This is the temple itself and it occupies the whole space up to the roof. Not only does this height give a sense of dignity and impressiveness to the place where the lodge performs its ceremonies but it permits the use of an original oak gallery, access to which is obtained from a small staircase leading to the dining room. This staircase is situated on the north side of the temple behind the Secretary's table. This gallery provides some 10 places for those not able to find a seat downstairs and to protect those who mount there and may possibly be overcome with vertigo an iron rail has been provided to enable those on the front row upstairs to stand to order in greater safety. The gallery was used in early days by the lodge choir made up of Stewards and those with choral ability. Latterly it has been used as an organ loft but now that a new organ has

Left: *The pillars in the west with gallery visible above the seating.* Above: *Looking east.*

been installed on the temple floor, the extra seats are of advantage especially during Installation ceremonies.

To return to the floor of the temple, the scene is one of distinct antiquity. This is provided by the dominance in the room of the two large pillars with cream shafts and gold pedestals and chapiters. Those pillars are surmounted by two globes, terrestrial and celestial, each covered by lace giving a realistic impression of the two great pillars mentioned in the second degree tracing board. They are of the Tuscan order and actually supported the pulpit in the clandestine chapel from which John Wesley preached during his visits to the town. The fact is substantiated by a brass plaque affixed to 'that on the left'.

The chairs in the lodge room give a remarkable sense of harmony and yet were produced more than 100 years apart. In 1869 a Bro Richardson reported that he had seen seven chairs suitable for the lodge at Bristol and that the price was £11. He proposed that they be bought forthwith and a Bro Chapman seconded. This was agreed. Hence one sees the chairs at the Officers' places with their fine carving and ample seats. However, the range of chairs that face one down the temple from the dais and the 3 English oak pedestals, that stand *before* the Master but *to the side* of the Wardens' places, were only presented in 1945. These were a gift of Bros Gerald and Giles Holbrow and are of hardly less exquisite design and workmanship. The pedestals were made from oak selected by the donors, cut in their own mills at Bradford-on-Avon and fashioned at the hand of an expert craftsman in Bath. Bro Giles Holbrow remarked on the day of their presentation that although the trees from which the new pedestals were made had only been recently felled it was not impossible that the age of the wood in them was even greater than that of the timber from which the rest of the hall was constructed. A plate is affixed to the Master's pedestal describing the gift.

The tracing boards, which are in a light oak cabinet, were gifted in 1907 and are of a slightly different nature in that they are joined in a triangular format on a central swivel and set in such a manner that they can be revolved within the cabinet by the index finger bringing the appropriate one to the top as required. They are covered by a removable oak panel when closed.

Adding even further to the appearance and sense of antiquity here are the two fine globes that appear on a ledge behind the Master's chair. They are in the low cradles which usually held such items in the study or library of all learned gentlemen in the seventeenth century and they bring to life those same features on the present Grand Lodge certificate. Between them, as shown in the picture from the gallery, there are three very old candlesticks, a pot of incense used in earlier forms of Craft/Royal Arch ceremonies, and a cabinet of masonic jewels, one or two of which are of special interest.

Together with the dark oak wooden pews used by the brethren and the charming south window renewed and dedicated to the memory of WBro A. Wallington, the lodge's generous benefactor, one has here a fitting climax to a hall that does Bradford-on-Avon and its masons proud. It is a matter for rejoicing that not only did the members find the sums necessary for yet again restoring this unique hall in two years (1967–69) but that they are still prepared to work hard to maintain their heritage. Mr Horton would have been proud of them.

BRIGHTON

The Home in Queen's Road

PRIOR TO 1852 there were three lodges which were recorded as meeting in Brighthelmstone in the county of Sussex. The earliest of these does not appear to have left any trace of its having worked but the other two began in the period when the re-named Brighton was becoming a large and fashionable seaside resort. One of them, the 'Royal Clarence' was named after one of the Prince Regent's brothers whilst the other, 'Royal York', was given a similar royal connection when it transferred from Seaford where it had met as the Royal Cinque Port lodge for 25 years. Their residence at the Old Ship and White Horse hotels respectively effectively ensured that from this time Brighton became the heart and centre of Freemasonry in the county.

The upper processional corridor at Brighton.

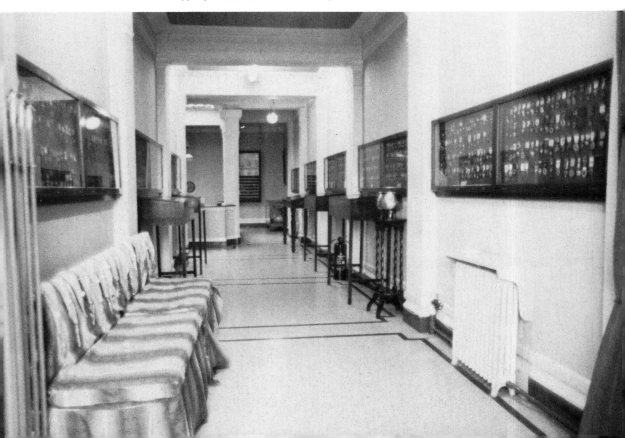

The advent of the royal and many less distinguished visitors to the town was considerably helped by the new provision of Macadam roads both from London and to other seaside areas and by 1841 the railway station was in place and the London and Brighton Railway was operating. The steady and significant increase in the local population meant that there had to be a comparable provision of new houses and it was a brother of considerable financial means and some masonic importance whose name is still associated with an area of the borough that emerged at this time. His name was Thomas Read Kemp.

Born in 1772, the son of the MP for Lewes, he married a daughter of Nicholas Baring, a banker, and her marriage portion, added to what he inherited in 1811 from his father, made him a quite wealthy man. In 1819 he built a house in Montpelier Road which was supposed to have been designed to the measurements of King Solomon's Temple and which is now the Brighton and Hove High School for Girls. His interest in the Temple of King Solomon is hardly surprising for he was initiated in the Royal Clarence Lodge in 1804 and was made a joining member of South Saxon Lodge, Lewes (see elsewhere in this volume) in 1821. Interestingly he acted as a Past Master at the laying of the foundation stone of the Lewes Gas Works in 1822 yet it was only in 1823 that he was elected WM though he had not yet served as Warden. Steps were clearly taken to obviate this lack for in 1824 he became the Master of South Saxon Lodge and in 1830 was appointed Deputy Prov. Grand Master by the 5th Duke of Richmond.

During this time as Master of the Lewes Lodge he embarked on his most ambitious scheme of land development by constructing what has been called 'one of the finest examples of Regency architecture and planning in the country'. The scheme was an overambitious one but it has meant that Kemp Town is still a well known part of East Brighton and it is hardly surprising that one of the first names

The main temple, another with illustrations of the Zodiac on the ceiling.

that a visitor to the present Masonic Hall in Queen's Road will see is that of this operative as well as speculative mason.

The earliest recorded meetings of the Provincial Grand Lodge in 1817 and 1823 were held in the Assembly Rooms and the Royal York Lodge also moved there in 1859. In 1858, however, the Brighton lodges appointed a committee to investigate and report on the possibility of erecting a masonic hall in Brighton and not only did the ensuing report claim that the venture was financially viable but it was suggested that a masonic library, museum and banqueting facilities should also be contemplated. The idea was 'contemplated' but nothing was done. Ten years later the renovated Royal Pavilion, which had been stripped of its finery at Queen Victoria's command, was available for masonic hiring and both the Royal Clarence and the Provincial Grand Lodge were to meet there for 80 years.

From the desire to have a separate masonic temple there did develop the idea of a club room where the growing numbers of brethren and their guests could meet informally and after a short stay at Regent House, on the corner of New Road and Church Street, a site was leased in 1897 at the present 25, Queens Road and HRH the Duke of Connaught and Strathearn laid the foundation stone of the present Sussex Masonic Club premises. The lease was for 21 years so the end of the First World War brought a threat of closure. At a meeting of Provincial Grand Lodge on December 17th that year WBro William Porter, Prov SGW-designate made the offer that if the brethren would raise £5000 to purchase the club premises and the six cottages adjoining and present it to the Province he would 'at his own expense erect thereon a building comprising two lodge rooms with all necessary accommodation and offices for the Provincial Grand Secretary, this being as a memorial to his only son killed in the war'.

This offer was accepted with the greatest appreciation. Trustees were appointed and the site purchased and a contract was entered into immediately to lay the floor of the entrance hall and prepare such part of the foundations as would permit a foundation stone to be inserted. This was duly laid with full masonic rites on 26 June, 1919. Provincial Grand Lodge being opened and closed in the adjoining Masonic Club. In the event it was not as easy to progress with the alterations to the property as had at first been supposed because the adjoining cottage tenants had to be re-housed before work could go ahead. When, in 1924, the work could begin in earnest WBro Porter died and so never saw the result of his generosity come to fruition. He had personally handed over £10,000, that being the amount estimated for the building cost. In the end some £17,000 was needed with £5000 for the site and further thousands of pounds for the furnishings. At length, on 20 July, 1928, the Provincial Grand Master, MWBro the Rt Hon Lord Ampthill, attended with a team of senior Grand Officers to dedicate the building for masonic purposes. The building was designed to integrate with the existing club premises, and in recent years the properties on both sides of No 25 have also been purchased to permit extention should circumstances so require. Brighton masons at last had a home of which they could be rightly proud.

It is hard today to realise that this hall was once the normal home of a Brighton gentleman. Very recently there has come to light the diary of John Hill Kidd, Esq, of Windsor House, Queen's Road, Brighton and we are beginning to uncover something more about the previous life of these premises. The fine Doric pillars that proudly flank the porticoed doorway of the Sussex Masonic Club must have once impressed the passers-by with the status of the occupier and now have the same impact on those who may wonder what lies within.

The main entrance to the temple is in fact slightly to the right on the spot where one of the adjoining cottages must have stood. Above the double doors with their beacon-type lanterns we read the clear description 'MASONIC TEMPLE'. It is by this entrance that most visitors will pass when they come to a Brighton lodge and as they enter they will at once realise what an impressive change has overtaken the original domestic interior.

Facing the doors and across a marble-floored entrance hall of lofty proportions there rises a wide and richly decorated stone staircase. It leads, as we shall see, to the first landing at the foot of a spacious well that then stretches upwards to the very roof of this three-floored building. At the top of the well is a glass ceiling and with this the well and staircase are clearly lit during the day and no less well illuminated in the evening.

Before we ascend the staircase, however, we shall do well to look at a few of the items that are disposed about the ground floor and the lower temple which leads off to the left just beyond the foot of the stairs. There is, for instance, just within the entrance itself a most significant if somewhat seat-worn Master's chair that once belonged to the Royal Clarence Lodge but is now placed here for safe keeping. It is a chair of most ample proportions, some four feet between the arms, with a tall, spacious back framed between two carved pillars. These pillars are capped with two globes, each one foot across, and representing in wood the celestial and terrestrial spheres. They revolve on their fluted bases and to distinguish them correctly the celestial globe has a diagonal band of Zodiac characters, whilst the terrestrial globe has clearly defined longitudinal markings. The chair is a fitting introduction to the treasures of this Sussex temple and by its unprotected presence here shows at once that this hall has no hidden museum but is full of masonic delights in every part of the building.

Moving then into the lesser temple to the left, past the steps and corridor that now join the entrance hall to the older Masonic Club rooms and bar, we find ourselves in a complex of three smaller rooms with a host of historic items on the walls of each. Here one will see a diagram explaining the geographical lay-out of the 12 Tribes of Israel, an exquisitely carved mirror with almost every known pre-Union Craft and Royal Arch motif, and a rare collection of Harris tracing board miniatures with the inclusion of two Royal Arch designs, one of which is rarely if ever seen today. This framed collection is signed by the donor 'John Mellor, 1838' but the collection seems to be one of a contemporary series prepared by John Harris himself in 1813. The first of the Royal Arch boards is identical with one mentioned in the visit to Newport (see elsewhere in this volume) but the latter would appear to be the kind of presentation that sank without trace at the Union of the 2 Grand Lodges.

In this suite of rooms there is also a set of early Rose Croix aprons, a panel explaining the story of the Amity biscuit (see the chapter on Poole), and a simple but instructively designed black and white apron of about 1784. Indeed, the contents of but this part of the Brighton Masonic Hall would constitute a matter for remark in many other masonic meeting places. It is but a presage of so much else that awaits us above.

Let us then mount the stairs and look first at the two display cases that confront

us on the landing. In the first of these a recent addition has been a plate (one of three only), made to commemorate the first landing on the moon by brethren Neil A. Armstrong, Edwin E. Aldrin, Jnr and Michael Collins. It was a personal gift from a brother from the Potteries to the present curator. This is flanked by two charming china Mopses with masonic Masters, a crib of silver presented to a 1904 WM whose year in the chair coincided with his becoming a father, a curvy sword such as was once the implement held by the tyler at the door of the Lodge (itself a symbolic reminder of how an angel guarded the entrance to Eden with a flaming one), and a jewel for the 1897 Festival, in the year of Queen Victoria's Jubilee to adorn the breast of a lady steward.

To the right of these cases, full of so much more glass and pottery, there is at the foot of the next flight of stairs a case with three very delicate and rare Chapter jewels of about 1810. The centre one of these was obviously that of the MEZ but as to which of the other Principals the other two belonged is a matter that still needs a measure of masonic enquiry. Below this trio there is a watch in the form of a keystone and alongside that an Irish apron of 1799.

Mounting the stairs we pass on our left an apron of the Orange Order, some elaborate German jewels, an Antients apron of the Lodge of Justice dated 1816, and one of those large handkerchief charts that are themselves a source of intense masonic interest for any enquiring student. We have now reached the Provincial Grand Master's room and, if vacant, this too is well worth entering.

In the centre here is a fine mahogany table surrounded by beautifully carved chairs. One of this set is laid aside at the end of the room, in front of a decorated glass-bookcase, and is designated the Kingston Chair because it belonged to the Earl of that name. The chair is of the Queen Anne period and had belonged to the Earl of Kingston, a friend of George II, who died in 1764. The chair then belonged to the family of J. P. M. Smith for 120 years before passing to the Royal Clarence Lodge in 1889. Sadly, excessive pressure on its back has slightly damaged its scroll work and it is now for viewing only. As a set the chairs richly adorn this mini-museum, for that is what it is. A glass case near the door has a host of minor masonic treasures—a portable baton light used by military lodges, a rare silver gilt trowel worn by the tyler (as is still the case in Royal York Lodge No 315 here), three exquisitely decorated snuff boxes, an Apron of 1768, 2 large pottery Mauls with fascinating designs on their sides, a miniature desk containing both a VSL and a copy of the Koran, again for military lodge use, and several other pieces of decorated pottery.

We again mount the stairs that surround the centre well and immediately notice the special apron (Prinny's pinny) worn by George IV on a ceremonial occasion at Brighton, a display of gold jewels of the Scottish Constitution, including one with a Corinthian pillar at right angles to the segment of a circle—the jewel of a Scottish Grand Architect. Here too we see another well painted apron of about 200 years ago and then a large case of many Craft, RA and Mark jewels, amongst the latter of which we see examples of the plug form which preceded the present keystone design.

The old Master's chair of Royal Clarence Lodge. The portrait is of William Porter.

We are now at the top of the building and passing along a well-lit corridor towards the main temple. Cases of further historical objects line the marble passageway and again the contents are too numerous to detail in full. Two folding light brackets used by military lodges, a horn bookmark or shoehorn covered with much symbolic detail, and a five-sided heavy metal plate with Mark lettering around it are just a few of the strange and unexpected items that can be gazed at in this further addition to the hall's open museum whilst in the preparation room that faces the main temple door are other cases with choice jugs and basins all covered with masonic verses and insignia. The mug of 1775 and an indented border plaque of heavy iron (like the one mentioned in the hall at Lewes elsewhere in this volume) provide real matter for study whilst the officers' chairs in this room, though idly stacked, would do justice as historical pieces to many a lesser masonic meeting place.

We now pass at last into the main temple. It is very large and lofty with a most impressive centrepiece that looks like blue tinted glass in a low circular dome surrounded at the lower edge by panels each carrying one of the signs of the Zodiac. What will perhaps amaze the visitor to learn is that in fact the so-called 'glass' is in fact painted canvas and the strong-looking metal frames are but painted wood. It is a trompe l'oeil worth special notice.

Surrounding this lovely temple with its marble, chequered flooring is rich panelling with imposing chairs for the Senior and Junior Wardens. The Master's podium is surrounded by especially heavy woodwork and covered with a rich wooden canopy at the back of which is a light to reveal 'that bright morning star' and beneath it a panel showing the hand of the Almighty pointing down to where the Master sits. The whole room is an unexpected assembly hall seating up to 200 persons.

On the north wall, behind where the Secretary and Treasurer sit, there is a double-fronted cabinet made of wood with iron brackets. Herein are the three tracing boards which are revealed when the lodge is opened and slid to one side according to the degree being practiced. The painter of them is unknown but they are not of normal design. The first degree board has 3 pillars in line (rather like the ancient board at Faversham in this volume), the second has a building in blue with winding stairs that encompass it on both sides, whilst the third degree board shows a figure in shrouds actually lying in a deep recess, with the coffin lid lying partly to one side. The style, the use, the very positioning of these features only serve to convince the visitor that here is a masonic hall that one cannot easily overlook—a hall to remember.

The Master's chair in the main temple. Notice the divine hand and the bright morning star.

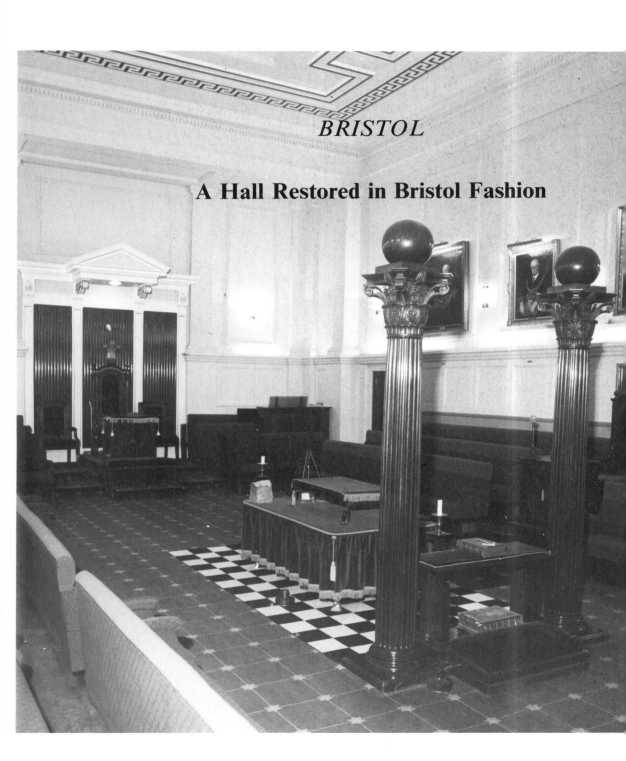

BRISTOL

A Hall Restored in Bristol Fashion

THERE CAN BE few Masonic Halls which have stood so firmly and so constantly at the heart of their cities as the one at Park Street, Bristol. Moreover there are no other halls that can boast as this one does that it houses not only all the lodges of its Province but all the other degrees as well. Yet, as with the history of masonry shown so clearly in the case of the other halls featured in this volume, the story of where freemasons should meet in Bristol has not been as straightforward as its apparent stability and continuity here would suggest.

At a Quarterly Communication held at the Bush Tavern on 25 February, 1812, it was stated that the cause of there having been so long a gap since the last such meeting was 'the very unsettled state in which the Lodges of the District had long been in, not from any neglect or fault of the Masters, Officers and Brethren of those lodges but from the cause of the extreme unpleasant and harassing treatment they had experienced at the hands of some of the landlords of the Houses where the lodges were held, which houses were to them no longer the Sanctuaries of Peace, but were become the habitations, wherein there was no certain rest for the soles of their feet'. The time seems to have come when the brethren had to build a place for themselves. It was proposed that £25 shares should be offered and within no time at all the Secretary of the Provisional Committee was reporting a sum raised of £1500.

For the next four years they rented a 'well appointed and handsome apartment' at No 77, Broad Quay and this had an immediate effect on their reputation. A Bro Richard Smith wrote:

> This was an improvement in Masonic affairs as by the removal from the Taverns, the dangers of the Bottle were lessened, and the Brethren escaped those censures that had been too justly thrown upon them, when a glass was taken for the good of the House, all discretions of this kind being placed to the Score of Masonry, whereas in point of fact the Lodge was closed and all business at end before a cork was drawn.

The Brethren now meeting in this new premise were invited to furnish the temple and a 'Grand Stewards Lodge' was formed to prepare the hall and also take care of the Provincial dinner arrangements. At this time there were four 'Modern' lodges, The Royal Arch Chapter of Charity, and the Encampment of the 'Royal Orders' using the new premises. They 'camped' there for but a short time.

In 1816 the lease ran out and steps were taken to purchase No 12 (the centre house) in Bridge Street. The lodge room here was 33½ feet long and 26½ feet wide with a small gallery at the West end. This gallery had a railing 'composed of lyres interspersed with Masonic ornaments' and a symbolic clock in the centre. (See a reference to such a clock in the chapter on Barnstaple, or at Worksop in Vol III). An organ 'with 12 stops' (which had cost £300 in building by the late George Daubeny MP) was bought for 40 guineas, but required nearly £30 more to put it in order and set it in position. It is the one still in use in the present Craft temple and although it has none of the advantages of modern construction, it possesses a mellowness of tone that is always much admired. Its installation is but a pointer to the desire of the Bristol masons to have all things very good. The decoration and furnishing cost £2000!

Links between this property and the one in Park Street which is used today were the paintings (upon floor cloth) which adorned the ceiling, the 'Grand' chair of 1792 (still in use for the Worshipful Master) and its mahogany pedestal presented by Bro Brant, Past Provincial Grand Chaplain, and a 'beautiful carved eagle to help suspend the canopy from' supplied by a Mr William Stock. It is worth remarking that the handsome chair just mentioned was given over to the proprietors of the Bridge Street Hall by the Royal Sussex Lodge of Hospitality in return for two shares of the building. On being received it was given 'more stuffing' and covered with 'Royal purple Morocco leather'. The eagle was gilded at more than the expected expense and meant that 'good Scotch glass' had to replace the 'painted glass' that the Committee planned.

In April 1857 another salutary change was made in having one tyler and hall-keeper for the whole Province. Bro John Drew, a member of Beaufort Lodge, undertook the duties for £30 a year, and a pension of £20 a year was granted to Bro Cameron, their later hall-keeper, during his lifetime. He enjoyed it only short of two months and a picture of him was then subscribed by the brethren, as was one of John Drew later. That part of Bristol's masonic history is also retained by the pictures that still adorn the present hall.

In December 1864 a letter was read to the Hall Governors from the Rifle Headquarters' Company in which they were offered the premises at the top of Park Street, then occupied by the Bristol Library Company. This was declined for financial reasons and in 1870 the chance to purchase the Philosophical Institution at the foot of the same street became a possibility. It was not viewed with universal approval. One Bro Cowlin, an experienced builder, is reported as saying, 'Fools build houses and wise men live in them'. He seems to have been wanting a new commission.

The entrance in Park Street, Bristol.

The Trustees of the Institution wanted a public sale, which meant that the freemasons paid some £500 more than the offer first made, but by April 1871 the purchase was complete.

When the hall was dedicated the upstairs portion was practically the same as it is today but the downstairs was completely different. The basement was at first let to a wine merchant but is now a well appointed kitchen. The Lecture Theatre was floored over to make a dining room and a proper water system was laid on in 1882 instead of the practice of drawing from the well on the premises. In 1889 the first banquet took place in a dining room fitted with boards that contained the names of all the PMs. These of course were destroyed in the burning of the hall during the blitz of World War II though they are now replaced with most exquisitely drawn panels on the walls themselves. In 1893 electric lighting was introduced, the

The Chapter room looking east.

cloakroom below stairs was constructed and in 1898 the chapel was thoroughly re-decorated and generally improved.

Today, after having suffered the greatest trials and tribulations through two world wars and having been very extensively damaged in 1942 the masons of Bristol can take great pride in what has been restored as their one and only temple.

The exterior of the hall has not changed through the years. It was first opened for use by the public in 1823, was intended as a museum, and for exhibitions of art, as well as lectures on Science, and other academic subjects. Over the doorway, therefore, and beneath the portico, is an allegorical frieze, carved and presented by Bro E. H. Baily, RA, FRS, who was born in the city in 1788. It was this same brother who sculpted the fine statue of HRH the Duke of Sussex at Freemasons Hall, London. It can be well imagined that an allegorical item dealing with the Liberal Arts and Sciences is well suited to stand at the entrance of the Masonic Hall.

On entering the building, apart from being carefully and courteously scrutinised by a commissionaire, one is immediately aware of the elegance of the structure. The semi-circular entrance hall, leading on the left to the basement with its ample cloakrooms, Grand Officers rooms, well-stocked and comfortable bar, and on the right into the reception foyer, is itself unusual and distinctive. The foyer is lofty and spacious with large settees on the right wall and desks for entering the names of visitors and members to the left. The tall marble pillars that support the roof with its classical lines, the glimpses beyond the desk of large and commodious dining rooms, and the elegant and wide staircase that rises at the far end to the next floor, all combine to give the visitor a sense of being admitted to a truly impressive building. The workmanship exhibited everywhere would have greatly pleased the brethren of a century or more ago who sought to have only the best for their use. The solid and well polished oak doors, the well chosen decorations, the wrought iron banisters, the marble treads—lead one to expect that what is said and done here is all of quality.

On the first floor landing one at first wonders where the various temples can be but this is simply a mark of the careful design. Behind the large but discreetly appointed doors are three extremely well-designed suites. One for the Craft, one for the Mark and one for the 'Royal' or 'Encampment' degrees. In each case the architects of the building have provided enough room for the forming of processions, the carrying out of special ceremonies (such as the Veils ceremony still attached here to the Royal Arch), and those many other tasks of preparation or extra dressing which Bristol masonry requires. Moreover, in addition to the ante-room space provided for the Craft temple there is an entirely separate and specially designed smaller temple, behind a normally locked door, in which the ceremony of conveying the secrets restricted to the Master's Chair is conducted. Those permitted to enter this other room will see something almost certainly unique in present day English masonry. The visitor will not be disappointed.

In the lay-out of the Craft temple certain elements that abound more in the west of England will be noticeable. Apart from the two miniature pillars that stand just within the temple entrance (and where the JD stands just before the lodge is opened to demand a password from those seeking to enter) the visitor will notice two other 10 foot high columns at the west end of the lodge carpet. These are permanent features and between them lies a long kneeling stool. Stretching

The Chapter room looking west with fine organ casing prominent.

eastwards from in front of the stool is a 12 foot long table covered with cloth and on top of the table is the plinth carrying the full-sized wooden tracing boards. Around the boards-case are the implements needed in the various degrees, together with a rough and smooth ashlar. In the Bristol lodge there is no tripod, but there are swords.

The Secretary and Treasurer occupy distinctive seats, the Secretary in the north-east corner and the Treasurer in the south-east, whilst the DC occupies a seat just to the left hand of the Master but below him, facing west. The Master's chair is raised up on a dais and in an alcove with the PGM's chair to the WM's right and the IPM's to the left. The Grand or Provincial officers sit in two rows facing west in the extreme NE corner and the PMs sit in a similar pair of rows in the oposite SE area.

The pedestal for the WM is to his right hand and not in front of him, whilst the main pedestal for the obligation is on the floor of the lodge at the foot of the dais steps. At the end of a small passage way to the left of the WM and in front of the PMs' rows is the door into the room for the Board of Installed Masters. The temple is otherwise of a neo-classical style, lofty and wide, with the large organ in the west end.

The 'Chapel' or room for the ceremonies of the Baldwyn Rite, including the Holy Royal Arch, is as lofty but of a smaller length and width than the Craft Temple. Here the Treasurer sits in the centre of the north wall with a specially designed seat and dais to enhance his position. The brethren who are equivalent to the Wardens sit with their backs to the same kind of 'west end pillars' which adorn all Bristol temples but here the pillars are decorated with 'Egyptian style' colouring and the whole decor of the room is of a fitting colour scheme. The graceful pipe organ at the west end is painted in white and blue and the organist is seated behind an 8-foot high panel against which sit the junior officers of the several degrees. The centre of the temple carpet is occupied with the same kind of table as elsewhere save that there is space for movement between itself and the pillars. The Chaplain has his own seat in the space used by the DC in the Craft room whilst the DC now sits in a place similar to DCs in other parts of England, the first row in the south east.

It can thus be seen that this hall has its own very distinctive traits. There remain two other parts of the hall which cannot be overlooked. The first is reached by taking one's way down a short corridor off the first floor landing. Passing two or three small but well-appointed rooms where candidates can prepare themselves for their various ceremonies in private and comfort we come to another of those gracious oaken doors—though this one has a noticeably gentle curve to it. Passing through you enter the PGM's private suite, a most charming circular room which you can realise is part of that same design as you encountered on entering the building. Here, with its gracious antique furnishing, one captures something of the style of the older Bristol hall which was destroyed in the war. It is a haven of peace fit for the leader of this Province and here too are kept the many essential items which Bristol has retained for ceremonies long since lost elsewhere.

On the floor above there is the new museum started afresh after the war when so much of historical importance was lost in the older museum on the ground floor. It was the war that removed many of the older minute books and records, and also some of the glass and china that others can still so proudly display. Yet here the

present curator is steadily building up a new collection and above all keeping that
record of the present which will be the meat and treasure of the masons yet to be
born. As one stands in this further part of the hall that has recovered so proudly
from the ravages of modern warfare one can only rejoice that Bristol masons have
such a fine heritage of ritual and practice that the hall that enshrines it is
recovering so rapidly a sense of 'Time Immemorial'.

The entrance hall with recording tables and display cases.

CANTERBURY

The Cathedral City Hall

As EARLY AS 1730 the first lodge to be constituted in Kent was formed at the Red Lion Tavern in the High Street, Canterbury. That first meeting date was 3 April and by Saturday, 20 May, its presence in the city led to the following proclamation by the Town Crier:

> Whereas a report runs through the city of an unlawful assembly of a number of men that meet together at the Red Lion Tavern in the City, and bind themselves under wicked obligations, to do something that may prove of sad effect, therefore the Mayor of this City desires that any person that can, to inform him aright, because the truth ought to be known, that such darkness be brought to light.

The lodge then met in the building next to the Guildhall and it appears that the door leading from the gallery in the Guildhall into the tavern was henceforth bricked up. How could the authorities guess that they were effectively 'tiling' the lodge next door! Since the Mayor in 1732 was a member of an Operative Building Guild it is hardly surprising if he was opposed to the new-fangled Speculative Masons Lodge.

By 1760 this Red Lion Lodge had ceased and the King's Head Lodge No 253 had been started. Connections with both these older bodies are still extant for in the museum which is attached to the present masonic premises we can see an 'Antients' Royal Arch tracing board that probably belonged to 253, whilst a still older three degree board comes from the Red Lion era. It seems most likely that the founders of the Lodge of Harmony, Faversham (whose present hall we are also displaying in this volume) were initiated in the King's Head Lodge. Within one year of constitution the members at Faversham had changed from being an 'Antients' to becoming a 'Moderns' lodge, unlike their Canterbury sponsors.

In 1863 there were three lodges meeting in Canterbury—United Industrious Lodge No 31 which incorporated the King's Head, St Augustine Lodge No 972 and the Royal Military Lodge No 1449, this latter being the only masonic lodge to have the right to carry the Royal Arms on its Past Masters' jewels. They had usually been separated by different meeting places in the city but by 1873 they all appear to have been using the Guildhall Hotel which was on one of the High Street corners.

The desire to have permanent premises for their meetings is shown by a number of Lodge 972 minute extracts of the time and in July 1878 there at last appears the following:

The WM proposed and Bro Miskin seconded that the lodge be removed from the Guildhall Hotel to 38 St Peter's Street. That 2 brethren be appointed to act in conjunction with lodges 31 and 1449 on the Building Committee to carry out alterations in the above building.

Four months later the same committee was being thanked by a Chapter for the 'effective and satisfactory manner in which they had adapted the building to Masonic purposes.'

Walking today down the street from the centre of the city towards the Westgate one would be hard put to it to distinguish the hall from the largely mediaeval buildings in which it is set. With its off-white plastered wall and graceful overhanging upper storey, not to mention its discreet and ordinary doorway, the visitor could only know his destination by the metal plaque that says simply,

Masonic Hall

Pushing on the door on lodge evenings the members then find themselves in a long corridor which once took people past the shop premises on the left—premises that were turned into the first lodge room here and which are now used as a place for rehearsal or for an overflow meeting when the main temple is occupied.

The corridor leads into an assembly area that once lay to the rear of the shop and which is now roofed over. Here the brethren can prepare themselves for entry into the temple and the inquisitive visitor will notice a framed picture of the historic stone-laying ceremony on 4th March, 1880 when by means of the usual large wooden tripod the foundation stone of the new temple extension was laid at its north-east corner in the garden of the older property in which the visitor is standing.

This extension had become necessary because by 1879 the restriction on space meant that ceremonies were having to be carried out in rapid succession. One evening records a complete third degree ceremony being at once followed by a triple first. Each of the three lodges involved agreed that further accommodation was required and undertook to support the plan to provide £450 for the necessary work. It was a formidable sum in those days, and it took a few years for the amount of a bank loan to be cleared by the brethren.

The actual stone-laying was carried out by the then Mayor of Canterbury, Bro J. Hemery (a pleasant reversal of local attitudes) and in the picture he stands prominently with his apron underneath his open coat! Alongside him one sees a brother whose name will ever be honourably associated with this hall, Horatio Ward, Prov GW of Wiltshire, who had now taken up residence in Canterbury and who was so obviously a competent and dedicated mason that he is here acting as Director of Ceremonies for the occasion. Interestingly he too has his apron underneath his frock coat.

The contract for the work had been placed with Bro Wiltshier of Lodge 31, who not only carried out the work to everyone's satisfaction but also carried a far from small share of the final £1000 funding of the hall. What was felt about him was shown by his being made an honorary member of the two other Craft lodges and by being suitably honoured in Bertha Chapter. They gave him his Chapter jewel and clothing. His efforts along with others were finally sealed by the temple being consecrated on 22 June, 1880 by Viscount Holmsdale (Baron Amherst), the RW Provincial Grand Master.

Before any brethren here pass into the very fine temple it is worth noticing two other features in the ante-room. The first is a charming mirror near the temple entrance. Its brightly gilded frame, with two small and elegant pillars, topped with small globes and network over them, at the sides, and representations of a smooth and rough ashlar, square and compasses at the base but with a coronet at the top centre, once held a Grand Lodge certificate, Mindful of the fact that this is not how such items should be preserved and yet not wanting to discard the piece the present curator of the hall's treasures had the certificate removed and the glass inserted and it now serves a most useful service in this robing area.

Alongside it and surrounding the doorway that leads into the temple proper is a very unusual feature. This is a solid Kentish oak surround which it is believed was originally the frame of the side door to the older building before the extension was erected. The presence of distinctive Tudor rose symbols and the general look of the item do suggest that it is a piece of sixteenth century carving. The small oak head of a Knight Templar at the centre of the cross lintel was added about 1978.

We thus pass into the temple, albeit pausing for a short time while in the tyler's area that separates the 'Tudor frame' entrance from the temple doors proper. Here you will be struck by a display of Knight Templar swords, helmet and breastplate. These remind us that the Black Prince Preceptory of Knights Templar No 146 was consecrated here on 10 June, 1880 and the first Em. Preceptor was none other than Horatio Ward who was then the proprietor of the Fountain Hotel. He is even more personally recalled in this small area by the presence on a shelf of a large silver cup and silver-plated salver which are used in the Knight Templar ceremonies and which were his personal gift to the hall. We shall also notice on the floor of the temple itself a silver and ivory-handled trowel which was given by Mrs Horatio Ward in loving remembrance of her husband.

Furthermore, as we are now in the temple area, we should notice, over the seat occupied by a Preceptor in a Knight Templar Preceptory, a replica of the Black Prince's shield, copied from the original which is over the Black Prince's tomb in the nearby Cathedral. This too was a gift from Horatio Ward.

The other shields that adorn this room add to its dignity and distinction and two of them portray the arms of HRH the Prince of Wales (later King Edward VII), and of Viscount Holmsdale, uncle of the late Lord Cornwallis, respectively. The shields, moreover, are enhanced by the impressive stalls that almost wholly clothe the eastern end of the building and which give a distinctly ecclesiastical look to the temple.

The canopied stalls were built by Bro John Greenhall of Lodge 31 in 1883 and were erected by the John Wiltshier who was the builder. Many brethren contributed to their cost and indeed it was hoped that in due time the whole temple would be surrounded by these attractive features. The centre two canopies in the east cover a space in which is set either the WM's chair for the Craft or an altar for the Preceptory. The Wardens' chairs stand, of course, outside the rows of stalls but are, as in certain other Halls, set with the SW on two steps, the JW on one step whilst the WM is in fact on a dais of three.

The chairs for these principal officers are themselves worthy of attention. They are three of a set of six which were presented by WBro Beer of 972 and his son and

The east view of the temple with distinctive stalls and the KT window.

are made from oak salvaged from a fire at the Cathedral in 1872. The Master's chair has an upturned square above its padded back, the SW's has a large gilt crescent moon with a face, and the JW's has a full orbed and faced Sun with rays. Seeing these reminds a visitor of the similar features over the chairs in the temple at Sunderland (See vol III of this series).

The oak pedestals which were bought in 1863 to serve the lodge 972 in the original front temple are still there for use in the LOI but the similar oak candlesticks were transferred to the new temple and stand beside the pedestals of lodge 31 that are used today. These candlesticks are of exceptionally fine design. Furthermore, the impressive and weighty brass columns that lie or stand upon the Wardens' pedestals are hollow, as the 2nd degree tracing board describes for the originals.

Another most distinctive feature of this temple, albeit one we have noticed elsewhere, is the fine pair of globes which stand upon elegant quadrupeds in the north-east and south-east angles of the temple. They were once placed upon the two small pedestals that are still flanking the WM's chair in the Craft but latterly they were set upon two four-foot high cast-iron pedestals which form part of the original heating system of this hall. The celestial globe was made in 1812 by T. Harris & Son of Gt Russell Street, London and bears a cartouche which reads:

> "Improved Celestial Globe". 'The stars laid down to
> the year 1820'. 'The days of the average of the
> leap years for 50 years to come'.

The terrestrial globe is by the same makers but has no date.

The warrants on the upper east wall spaces are of interest for that of Lodge No 31 is a 'Warrant of Confirmation' or 'Continuity' and is dated as 1806 for No 24. The St Augustine Lodge No 972 warrant was granted as 1274 in 1863 when it was consecrated by a Bro John Savage, PSGD of England, who was a PM of Athelstan Lodge No 19 which meets at Sion College, Blackfriars, London. There is here also the warrant of the Bertha Royal Arch Chapter No 31. It was this Chapter which reintroduced the Royal Arch to Canterbury following the demise of the Chapter of Concord No 38 around 1803. It was Bertha Chapter which received from Lodge 31 the RA tracing cloth of 1765 that was mentioned above and which used to hang behind the Inner Guard's chair until it was removed for safe keeping to the museum next door. Its original position reminds one of the Chapter board still hanging in the west at Faversham.

Before the opening of the present temple this Bertha Chapter met at the Guildhall Concert Rooms and it was from there that there came the attractive kneeling stool used by initiates today in this hall. It was presented by WBro Capt Philip Knight, WM of Lodge No 31 in his year as Master (1874/5).

In the centre of the lodge room when Craft ceremonies are performed lies a large oak plinth which contains the much valued tracing boards of Lodge 31. These were presented to the lodge 'by the brethren of the Elias de Derham Lodge No 586 of Salisbury as a mark of their very high esteem and regard for WBro Horatio Ward' and also 'in appreciation of all his many services rendered to Freemasonry in general, and to Elias de Derham lodge in particular'. Their gift was in June 1880 and they are signed 'F. Highman, Sarum'. Besides these tracing boards there stand the rough ashlar, the tripod with the smooth ashlar and the silver trowel.

This Hall is blessed with two different organs. In the original meeting place alongside the entrance corridor there is an 'American' organ which is still in working order and which served the brethren well when the room was the principal temple. In 1935, however, Bros Amos and Biggleston presented the very fine instrument which now occupies the south-west corner of the new temple. It was first constructed in 1789 by Hugh Russell of London and it is recorded as the 34th of its type in the archives of the Victoria and Albert museum. There are only three in this country 'in original condition', blown by an electric motor, with a light and mirror on the console. The brethren who kindly gave it to the lodge purchased it at a sale room in Tenterden for ten pounds. It had come from the Old Meeting House in that village and after being reconditioned at Brown's Organ Works in Canterbury it has become what it appears to be—a true collector's piece.

Before we leave the temple with its lofty wooden arch beams and stained glass windows at the east end we should not overlook the other stained-glass item on the south wall just above the Junior Warden's chair. Illuminated in its case on nights when the KT Preceptory meets it shows the figure of a mediaeval knight in full armour and with a royal surcoat. The figure is in fact wearing the arms of the Black Prince as can be verified by comparing them with the shield in the stall at the east. It must be an intriguing feature when nothing but the candles are lit, and only one factor disappoints Em Kt Hammersley who is the ardent and conscientious curator of these premises. On more careful examination one sees that the knight is actually standing in a reverse position to the norm. The trouble of changing round the glass and its lighting is too great to warrant the correction and its effect is in no way impaired.

Apart from yet another practice room, and the dining room above which will seat some 120 brethren, the last remaining asset of this hall is its quite large and well-stocked museum. Space in this chapter will not allow a detailed coverage of the museum's items but it would repay any mason with a keen interest in glass, medals, aprons, Kentish masonic portraits or a desire to know more about the Cornwallis family to stop for a couple of hours and browse in this well arranged display. The features that must be recorded here are some very large and well-framed RA and Craft tracing cloths, some intriging masonic handkerchiefs with abundant pre-Union symbols and a number of original collecting or ballot boxes from the lodges that have met here. A maul from the step-pyramid of Sakkara is one most original item, especially when you learn that it formed the pattern for the type of maul used at the laying of the foundation stone for the present Freemasons' Hall in Great Queen Street, London. When to all this you add a well-stocked and catalogued library you appreciate that here is a hall worthy of this ancient Cathedral city.

The globe on its stand.

CHELTENHAM

An Ancient Cotswold Temple

FOUNDATION LODGE, No 82 which first created and now continues to occupy the Cheltenham Masonic Hall, was first constituted as Lodge No 226 on 5 March, 1753. It first met, however, at Burton's Coffee House, Crane Court, St Peter's Hill, Doctor's Commons, just south of St Paul's Cathedral in the City of London and subsequently moved as No 127 to the Freemasons' Coffee House in Great Queen Street. It is of interest to note that in 1775 one of its members was Bro Alexander McKowl, described as a 'bricklayer', and it was largely as a result of this brother's advice that the site for the first Freemasons Hall in London was acquired and he became the contractor for the brickwork in its erection. Most of the master craftsmen employed in building the hall became members of the Lodge, and it was probably in May 1775, shortly after the laying of the foundation stone, that the lodge was named 'The Foundation Stone Lodge', changed later in that year to its present title of 'Foundation Lodge'.

In 1807, the lodge, then No 96, removed to Abingdon in Berkshire, and at the time of the Union of the Grand Lodges in 1813 was renumbered yet again as No 121. It was during its sojourn there that the lodge seems to have gained many members of rank and opulence for among the forty-seven who were added to its ranks there were two peers, a baronet and three Members of Parliament as well as nine Mayors of the town. The Church and the professions were well represented also and one of its members, Sir John Throckmorton, who had been Prov GM for Buckinghamshire from 1796, was appointed Prov GM for Berkshire from 1817 until his death in 1819.

On 1 July, 1817, the lodge was granted a 'Warrant of Confirmation' and made its final removal to Cheltenham in August of that year. The lodge grew rapidly in numbers and in strength and one of its first honorary members was Dr Edward Jenner FRS who was so closely associated with the development of vaccination. The lodge met seven times in 1817, 19 times in 1818 and thereafter it was quite normal to have more than a dozen meetings in a year. Within a year of the move to the town, on 5 August, 1818, it was proposed by Bro Thomas Josephus Baines (WM in 1832) that the lodge should build its own hall. Ground at the junction of Portland Street and Albion Street was purchased for £670. Bro G. Underwood, the architect of Holy Trinity Church, was asked to prepare plans and estimates, and the estimated cost of the finished structure was £2,200. It was occupied on 5 November, 1823, and became one of the very small number of purpose-built halls which have been continuously occupied since that time.

East and west views of the temple with gallery in the west.

Originally freestanding, the façade of the building is most impressive for what is otherwise a very modest street, and yet it is not easy for the newcomer to appreciate at first the frontage which runs almost up to the narrow pavement. A simple iron fence divides the hall entrance from the road and it is only by crossing to the other side of the street that one can appreciate the plain but dignified lines of the superstructure. At ground level a string of rusticated stonework is pierced by two round arched entrances, one of which is no longer used. Above these doors are two large round-arched niches which have yet above them two entablatures showing an inverted square on which lies an open VSL with a square, compasses and plumbline again superimposed. Between the niches is a large recess with its own very imposing round arch and on the front face of the building, flanking the arch, are two plain columns with unusual capitals seemingly meant to depict network, lilywork and pomegranates. The whole façade is completed with a pediment and frieze above which stands an oblong block resembling a fluted chimney top. It was originally flanked by two ornamental vases now demolished. The whole edifice stands sharply above the line of the adjoining shops and houses and when properly regarded makes a striking impression.

On entering the building through the right-hand, ground floor door one realises the antiquity of the premises. It is not at all surprising to learn that we are seeing the original hall plan, virtually unchanged. The entrance hall is simple but gives a sense of warmth and intimacy which is enhanced by the dark blue pastel shade of the wall decoration and the attractive winding staircase that leads up from the hallway to the ante-room and temple above. One is aware of a Regency elegance and tastefulness that must have been both required and enjoyed by those first users of this building.

Below where we are standing is a basement with kitchens. It would seem that these or the banqueting room to our left may not have been complete by the time of the first opening, for we read that after the first lodge meeting the brethren dined at the Vittoria Hotel in Liverpool Place and that 'the wines were good, many appropriate toasts were drunk and the evening was spent in great conviviality'. Good as that accomodation seems to have been it is in this present hall that all refreshment was taken thereafter.

It is into the room in which so much refreshment and pleasure was enjoyed that we ought first to turn our steps. To put this very distinctive part of the building in context we need to learn a little more about the development of Freemasonry in Cheltenham.

'The Foundation Chapter of Unanimity', attached to the lodge, was constituted in 1824, seven Foundation Lodge members having been exalted in the Chapter of Hope and Sincerity of the Royal Lodge of Faith and Friendship at Berkeley, Gloucestershire in June 1819. By October of that year five of those Royal Arch masons had been accepted as Knights Templar in the very ancient Knight Templar Camp of Baldwyn at Bristol which had already been working its seven degrees for many years. It was because of these steps that the way was open for the establishment of Knight Templary in Cheltenham as well.

On 8 August, 1833, Bro Mordaunt Ricketts, an enthusiast for this order, called a meeting for the foundation of a Coteswold Camp, and a further ten Royal Arch masons were proposed for membership. In the meantime a Warrant had been granted and the Coteswold Encampment was consecrated by Sir Knight John

Christian Burckhardt, Deputy Grand Master of the order at this Cheltenham Hall. The officers' titles will indicate to some the antiquity of this new Knight Templar unit—Mordaunt Ricketts was the first Commander, he had two Captains, a Prelate and an Expert and a Captain of Lines. The local paper reported the event with the news that 'the proceedings finally terminated with a banquet provided for the occasion in the Refectory'.

There is no doubt that the banqueting hall into which we now step today was used as the refectory of those Knights Templar. It was they who carried out the elaborate decoration of the walls and ceiling of this room and they could encounter no administrative problems in doing so for all the officers were also Past Masters of Foundation Lodge.

Originally the ceiling was painted to represent the roof of a tent, with lines resembling canvas seams radiating from the beautiful six light chandelier in the centre. This part of the decoration was lost when the ceiling was repaired in July 1883 but a recommendation by the restoration committee to paint over the murals on the walls was rejected by the brethren of Foundation Lodge who wished to retain the old style.

The main entrance to the dining room is through double doors in the west, beautifully panelled within a classical architrave. The north wall is painted to represent wooden stalls, in each of which hangs a shield bearing a colourful blazon of arms. It is thought that this design owed something to similar designs in the old Baldwyn Camp at Bristol which was unhappily destroyed during World War II. Over one of the doors leading to the kitchens below there is depicted the closed book of the Holy Gospels on a rich plum-coloured cushion, the book having the 8 pointed star of the Baldwyn rite embossed on its cover. Over the other door is a representation of the Paschal Lamb, the emblem both of Christianity and of the Templar Order.

The ancient 'refrectory' with shields and 'stalled' decoration.

The east window has on either side the painted recumbent figures of knights, one with crossed feet resting on a lion, indicating that he had died whilst on Crusade; and the other with a hound at his feet, suggesting that he had returned safely to die a natural death at home. Both tombs are canopied and decorated with pennants of arms and the Vexillum Belli of the Templars.

On either side of the fireplace on the South wall are further stalls embellished with shields, and in the centre of the stone mantel-piece is a carved shield showing a Christian cross entwined by a snake, rising above a stone-built bridge over water—the insignia of the 5th degree of the Baldwyn Rite, the East of the Sword and Eagle. At each end is carved a shield with a peculiar device for which at present no known attribution can be provided whilst the cast-iron fire grate is ornamented with shields bearing Templar crosses. The mural above the mantel-piece was hidden for many years by a portrait of Sir Michael Hicks-Beach, later the first Earl St Aldwyn Prov GM for Gloucestershire 1880–1916, and himself a member of this Coteswold Preceptory. The murals we now see have their own story.

In 1980, nearly a century and a half after their decoration by the first Coteswold Camp, the ceiling and walls of this banqueting hall were in a sorry state. The cumulative effects of much tobacco smoke, the scraping of chairs and tables and the periodic incursions of damp had reduced the murals to but a shadow of their old originals. The hall committee, anxious though it was to try and preserve this unique room, seemed to have no alternative but to repaper or paint over the walls.

It was the brethren of Royal Union Lodge who undertook in 1981 to have the murals restored. The walls and ceiling were carefully cleaned and restored to something of their pristine form by a Miss Anita Lafford, an artist and sculptress, the daughter and sister of two Past Masters in Royal Union. Due to her great skill, dedication and care, the assistance of several brethren and a generous donation from the Great Priory one sees today the results of her labour. The banqueting hall is now as magnificent as when it was first conceived. Only one has to stand in it to be reminded of the vision of those first Knight Templars who created this glorious background.

To complete our tour of the room we should once again look at the west wall where there are more knights' stalls on each side of the entrance doors. Over the doors is painted a plumed helmet, and above this, on a riband, the motto 'Domine quis habitabit' from the 15th Psalm—'Lord, who shall abide (in thy tabernacle?)'.

Looking at the room as a whole one sees how the murals form a unique background to another knightly feature, the horseshoe-shaped mahogany dining tables, heavily pitted with marks of the old firing glasses, and which, when set with silver and glass, ashine and glittering in the light of the candelabra and the chandelier above still preserve for us a masonry that being old is still alive and well.

It was fitting that to mark the completion of the restoration of this part of Cheltenham Masonic Hall a plaque should be unveiled by RWBro Cyril Hollin-shead, Order of St John, PGM for Gloucestershire, and a Past Master of Foundation Lodge. This unique room is now enjoyed and admired by more than 500 Freemasons who belong to lodges and chapters which regularly meet at the hall.

It is time to mount the winding staircase with its slender banisters and gently rising steps and enter the main treasure of this hall, its temple.

The form and decoration of this lofty room has changed little since its completion some 164 years ago. The azure blue ceiling, gold starred, with a magnificent golden centrepiece, and surrounded by a beautiful frieze and deep coving, provide a constant reminder to the brethren of that description of the lodge 'as high as the heavens'. The tiny winding staircase in the north west corner leading to the balcony, with its beautiful wrought-iron work, backed by crimson velvet; the tiled and ornamented fireplace; and the two pillars at the porchway or entrance all form part of the original design.

Later, other attractive embellishments to the room were added or presented by members of the lodge. The portrait of St John the Evangelist which hangs over the fireplace, was presented to the lodge by Bro Baines on St John's Day in December 1827, this day having been prescribed as the date of the Installation Festival certainly from 1807 onwards, and as it is now. The attractive organ was presented to the Lodge at a similar festival in December 1832 by Bro Mordaunt Ricketts, and in 1834 the lodge erected, at a cost of ten guineas, the very impressive feature in the east; the long, red plush and domed canopy, inscribed 'Faith, Hope, Charity', that surrounds the dais and the Master's throne. Changes since that time relate only to carpetting and furniture, and the gradual addition of Honours boards and warrants which now form an integral part of the wall decoration.

The original mahogany chairs, that include one for the Master given by Bro Welch and a Warden's chair given by Bro Torre, are a most gracious set which earned the admiration of Sir Hugh Casson when he came to the Hall in 1941. Indeed he was so struck by the building that he wrote an article on the hall for the Architectural Review of that year. But the present Master's chair is not one of these. The throne beneath the canopy, and the Wardens' chairs, were brought to the Hall by Royal Union Lodge when they started to meet permanently at the Hall from 1854 onwards. These had probably been acquired from the old Royal York Lodge which had also met, like the Royal Union, at the King's Head in Cirencester in 1813 prior to the removal of Royal Union to Cheltenham in 1822. It is interesting to note how, like some masonic warrants in earlier times, the main pieces of furniture did service for more than one masonic unit over a number of years. In this case, as in so many others, it is to our benefit that we can see the skill and workmanship that went into producing these 'thrones'. The pedestals that accompany these chairs are also worth noticing, having been made and presented to the hall by a great and generous freemason, Bro Felix Miles, PAGDC.

In 1882 the renovation and redecoration of the temple was undertaken by the brethren of Foundation Lodge, under the direction again of Miss Lafford and with a liberal grant from the hall committee. The original border motif on the ceiling, which still survives from 1823, depicts the Anthemion, a Graeco-Roman floral representation of honeysuckle used by the famous Adams brothers in the 18th century. Honeysuckle was the emblem of fidelity, and the same representation is found on the balcony, with the lyre, and on the entrance gates to the hall. A Victorian dado round the temple walls also depicts this same honeysuckle design. As for the seating for the generality of the brethren the original plain benches with beautifully turned legs, to which ugly and uncomfortable backs had been added in the nineteenth century, have now been replaced by pews from a redundant Somerset church, almost contemporary in date with the hall.

Another feature worthy of remark is to be seen in the two slender columns, each bearing spherical balls, at the west end of the room and supporting the balcony above. That on the left is a terrestrial globe with simple names like the Southern and Eastern Oceans, while the other is decorated with mythical beasts and birds, one representing the constellations, thus pointing out masonry universal. One is reminded of the similar arrangements at Bath and Bristol though here the room is more intimate and homely. The ancient banner of Foundation Lodge, originally No 121 but altered in 1832 to No 97 Cheltenham, is also on display. With its sun, moon, stars, square and compasses in the FC position, the square, rule and level serves to recall once more the ancient nature of the Freemasonry that this hall has sought to retain.

Nothing finally remains to be noticed but some items related to 'refreshment' and which span the years since this hall came into use. In 1821 two presentation glass goblets were accepted by the lodge from Bro Henry Pointer. They are most delicately and fully engraved with a host of contemporary masonic symbols and the donor's name around the base, with a simple stem beneath. There are the No 121 firing glasses which were taken out of commission in 1913 when new glasses were brought. Certainly the earlier version could have made substantial indents to any table with their reinforced, five-fold bases. There remain, too, many items of the original Dinner Service purchased in 1823 and in constant use certainly until 1908. In the corner of the impressive banqueting hall and on a convenient side table stands the 'Initiate's Little Brown Jug', of substantial Doulton stoneware, 24 inches in height, which is figuratively filled with Cheltenham waters and offered to each newly-made brother at refreshment. The two bands of decoration on the jug show naked putti making much of the vine and then mounted huntsmen pursuing their prey. The double allusion, with vine or acanthus leaves above and below, must have delighted generations of masons who have supped in this hall. From this place many have gone out to pursue their daily avocations with new merriment and pride. This is indeed a hall to remember.

The initiate's little brown jug.

EXETER

Rising Like a Phoenix

The oldest lodge in the Province of Devonshire is St John the Baptist lodge, No 39 which has worked in Exeter since 1732. The lodge has had various names, Union (1768), St John (1769) and its final and present name from 1821. It had nine numbers up to 1863 and met in no less than 20 different locations. Some of these latter were quite intriguing—Bro Furlong's, Gandy Lane; Private Room, Theatre Lane; Public Rooms, London Inn Square; and the Phoenix Inn, High Street. By 1823 this lodge, like others in the city, was most eager to have its own home and led by St George's, No 112, which started a subscription list in that year, the other lodges and a chapter made a start on the sum needed to provide a hall of their own. There was also the desire to provide accommodation for the Provincial Grand Lodge. In 1841 St John the Baptist Lodge introduced a by-law offering life membership for five guineas in addition to the initiation or joining fee *or* three guineas extra for members of five years or more standing. This new money was to be deposited in the Exeter Savings Bank for the sole purpose of providing a masonic hall. Sadly the first negotiation for land proved abortive and the scheme was abandoned. Instead the lodges moved to Tuckers Hall in Fore Street Hill.

The Incorporation of Weavers, Fullers and Shearmen—known colloquially as Tuckers—had built their hall as a chapel in 1471 and had escaped confiscation at the Reformation by putting in an upper floor, thereby causing it to be deconsecrated. One brother who records the meetings in this hall said it was the most truly masonic apartment he had ever seen. It was 33 feet in length, three × seven feet in breadth and it was enriched with 33 shields, 33 banners and had 33 compartments in its beautiful roof. Not surprisingly the Exeter brethren felt comfortably accommodated.

Nonetheless there was a constant hankering after premises of their own but it was only 35 years later that the Gandy Street property was first mentioned in the lodges' minutes as an alternative to a site in Longbrook Street. The 2 lodges worked fast and within a matter of months had acquired the building at Gandy Street from a Mr Stone. The builders moved in to make the necessary alterations and on 23 April 1877 a special Provincial Grand Lodge was held and the present Exeter Masonic Hall was consecrated. Within 3 days the St John's Lodge had held its first regular meeting.

A tablet of Poltimore stone in the Gandy Street hall bears the following inscription:

THESE PREMISES WERE ACQUIRED AND ADAPTED FOR THE PURPOSES OF FREEMASONRY FOR THE EXETER LODGES IN THE YEAR 1876. THE LODGE ROOM WAS REBUILT IN THE YEARS 1895/6, THE FORMER ROOM HAVING BEEN DESTROYED BY FIRE. IN THE YEAR 1906 THE EXETER FREEMASONS' HALL COMPANY LTD. WAS FORMED WHEN THE REMAINDER OF THE PREMISES WAS RECONSTRUCTED AND FORMALLY OPENED BY R.W.BRO G. C. DAVIE, PGM, ON 5 SEPTEMBER 1907.

The building very soon became the centre of Devonshire Freemasonry and yet many of those who attend meetings in it are probably unaware of both its antiquity and its constant recovery through the years.

The striking entrance from the street was at one time the gateway into a small courtyard leading to the door of the residence of a well-known family of wine merchants. This family, the Grangers, lived both here and at Musgrave House,

carrying on their business in Gandy Street during the latter part of the 1600s and until the beginning of the eighteenth century. Although it was not then a masonic building as such there is evidence to show that Freemasonry was being practised in the house by brethren in their private capacities.

The entrance already mentioned was then marked by very fine central and side entrances with old oak screens and corbels which bore coats of arms. These, with the oak beams and panelling in the entrance hall across the courtyard, must have given the house a special character and charm and hinted at what was unquestionably a very comfortable city mansion. It is worth noting that when the premises were being reconstructed in 1906 a number of traces of the older work were discovered. Embedded in the plastered walls of the refreshment room was a fine oak screen from around the fourteenth/fifteenth century. It was preserved in its entirety. On the ground floor much similar work was also uncovered.

The unusual and intimate, domestic atmosphere of this hall is evident the minute you pass through the decorated entrance door and foyer. The glass roof marks the area that was once the courtyard and yet enables the visitor to feel that he is at once within the building. The dark wood panelling gives a sense of warmth and friendliness and the mason will be struck by two items that immediately indicate the age of the place. Immediately ahead of the entrance is a framed pre-union apron with its heavily decorated surface, and on the left is a display case full of medals and jewels. Amongst the more normal decorations that appear in such cases we have here two distinctive Knight Templar jewels, one worn by pre-1850 Mark Masons locally, and a delicate eighteenth century Craft jewel of pierced work showing the prominent Jacob's ladder.

Turning left from the entrance hall we enter what is now the bar. In what might seem merely to be a place for relaxation there are three items that should receive attention. One is an unusual tile that was obviously used in a chapter ceremony. It is vaguely reminiscent of the tile still used on the floor of the old lodge room at Lewes but its design is definitely that of the Royal Arch. There is also a picture which clearly refers to the two degrees but which is not known elsewhere, and by the bar itself is a framed remnant of the old lodge carpet that was destroyed by the air-raid that nearly removed these premises and their contents altogether.

In 1942 Exeter suffered what became known as the Baedeker raids. On the 4 May Mr and Mrs Cawse were steward and stewardess of the Hall when five incendiaries fell through the roof of the present building, and landed in a room which was prepared for a ceremony. Being trained as one of the first women fire-wardens Mrs Cawse had immediate access to water-stirrup pumps but she and her husband felt that the most important thing to do was to rescue as much of the masonic furniture as they could.

They took the Bible, regalia, masonic tools, columns and boxes to the vaults of the Queen's Hotel opposite. As they were making one of their journeys Mrs Cawse remarked that she would get some of her own clothes. Her husband's reply was immediate: "These first: what we have here is irreplaceable." Mrs Cawse says that she got the message.

At 4 a.m. with the All Clear sounded Mrs Cawse ran to a nearby group of

The old merchant's entrance way with display cases and an old apron.

firemen and persuaded them to come round into Gandy Street where the incendiaries were still burning the insulation that had been put in the temple ceiling. She pulled down curtains to protect the organ bought only 6 years before and as she did so one of the firemen came over to help saying: "Let me help. I am a member of Plymouth Lodge". To this day no one knows the name of that brother who helped to save the masonic 'home' that still stands today.

It was some years before the lodge room was restored and in the interim the present dining room was used for ceremonies whilst the billiard room became the spot for the festive board. It is this story of preservation that one needs to recall as that small piece of carpet stares one in the face. Around you is a veritable Phoenix that arose from the flames. One of its earlier meeting places may have been a presage.

The portrait of RW Bro Kneal oversees the lodge room and the Master's chair.

As a reminder again of the old house from which this hall took its rise there is on the right of the entrance area a room called the Whist Room or old billiard room. It is here that the hall shows off its pottery. Compared with the items to be seen in the other halls mentioned in this book it has nothing of very special importance but the array of pots and bowls and mugs does serve to underline the antiquity of the lodges that meet here and to connect us with an earlier age.

It is in the dining room that we have a link with that Tucker's Hall that was previously occupied by the Exeter freemasons. Here, as in Cheltenham, we see traces of the Knight Templary which was so much a part of late eighteenth and early nineteenth century, even in a Craft hall, for there are shields which denote its presence even at the social board.

It is worth recording here that it was a Devon man, albeit later Provincial Grand Master of Dorset, William Tucker, who, recalling the move of the Exeter masons to the Tuckers Hall (was this a coincidence?), once made clear that he regarded Knight Templary as part and parcel of the whole fabric of freemasonry. He is recorded as saying:

> As a Devonshire man, he was doubly proud in the contemplation, that in this city of his ancestors and where the arms which he had the honour of bearing, were still to be found, he had received the perfection of Christian Masonry . . . and he should feel also an imperative obligation to wear the jewels indicative of every order and degree which had been entrusted to him . . .

He did! He appeared on one occasion as Provincial Grand Master in the robes of a Knight Templar and the Grand Master of England dismissed him from his high office! Such might be a salutary but engaging reminiscence when we still see in this old Craft hall the marks of a Christian masonic order, with Bro Tucker's coat of arms on one of these shields.

It is on the mantelpiece of this dining room that we can also see an object that might not be what it seems. With a box-like base, two slender pillared sides, and a rainbow coloured arch across the top this is thought by those connected with the hall to be an older type of ballot box. It resembles almost the same item on the Secretary's table at Sidmouth. On the other hand it also resembles the 'arch' used by the freemasons of Newport in the Isle of Wight for instructing the candidate in the Royal Arch degree. Could it perhaps be that what we have here is a previous Royal Arch implement now turned into a ballot box and then discontinued in use when a more modern style box was used in the lodge? The matter is worth considering.

We now mount the winding stair to the lodge room above. What strikes one here is that in the narrow ante-room outside the lodge door are two very impressive Egyptian type pillars. On enquiry it appears that they originally stood within the lodge room and flanked the entry area. They were removed as being too large for the limited space in the temple and hence adopted the place we see them in today. What is so encouraging is that they were not wholly disposed of as one suspects other pillars elsewhere were. These pillars are dated from the mid-Victorian period.

The temple itself is not much more than a large cube. Its greatest treasure is in the set of principal officers' chairs that have been in use for more than 200 years.

WBro James Jerman, who was a prominent member of St John's Lodge a century ago and also an architect by profession, has left us a description of them which cannot be improved upon:

THE MASTER'S CHAIR

Standing 5 ft 11 ins in height, is made of Spanish mahogany delicately shaped and curved. The seat is on Cabriole legs, in front having paw bases clutching a ball of four toes, the back legs being plain. The arms have dwarf Doric columns decorated with twining foliage on the surface of the shafts. The back is composed of gracefully treated scroll and foliage, open-panelling attached to Corinthian columns by a flat iron panel . . . The overhead has, as a central feature, the Bible set on a scroll work of clouds and foliage above which . . . are branches of foliage probably intended for sprigs of acacia, of symbolic import. Shields surmount the Corinthian columns, on the one being carved a pair of compasses and on the other a square emblematical of the Master's office. Binding together the elements of the overhead portion is a ribbon on which is cut the motto *Hic pacem muto damus accipimusque vicissim* (Here we give peace to one another and in our turn receive it). The chair dates prior to the close of the eighteenth century.

THE WARDENS' CHAIRS

These are of similar character and construction as the Master's, and are each 4 ft $3\frac{1}{2}$ ins in height and the portions below the seat are similar to that of the Master's chair. The arms, however, have not the columns supporting them . . . the back panels have open carved panelling of similar character to that of the Master's chair, but of less size only. The sides and top of the back have moulded and curved outline, of the form so familiar in the construction of chairs in the Chippendale period. As central and terminating features the ribbons bearing inscriptions round gracefully over the corners—the inscription over the SW's chair is *AE lege sortitur insignex et imos* (The lot is cast by the principal of equality to the most eminent and to the lowest alike)—and the inscription of the JW's chair is "Ultra citraque nequit consistere rectum" (Afar and at hand one does not abandon rectitude).

On the spaces at the top of each chair are carved representations of ashlar walling, that to the SW's chair having the rough ashlar only, finished by a long gilded level, and that to the JW's having in addition, depicted on a structure of rough ashlar work, three courses of perfect ashlar wall. A short gilded plumb rule is set in the centre against the latter, its base resting on the levelled top of the rough ashlar work.

The pedestal in front of the Worshipful Master sometimes carries a VSL belonging to St John the Baptist lodge which is stamped with the lodge's name and the words 'Holy Bible' on the spine. Despite this the contents are of the Old Testament only, a fact which proved to be a revelation to the masons of today. There is no sign that the volume ever had any part of the New Testament writings. It must, of course, be recognized that the six other lodges meeting here use their own VSLs.

The gavel blocks on the three pedestals are marked St John 39 and on the second degree tracing board there is a picture of a lamb which is designed as if it

Opposite: *The intricately carved WM's chair.*

The Wardens' chairs.

were the same as on the Golden Fleece decoration (ie with hunched back and feet drawn together). It is most surprising to see this symbol on what is so very much an Old Testament representation. Unavoidable on the south wall is a huge picture of an early nineteenth century clergyman, the Rev William Carwithen. It is not surprising that he should be so prominently displayed for he was of real local importance. He was initiated in St George's Lodge in January 1820, was soon made WM and held that office for 12 years between 1820 and 1835. From 1830 to 1850 he was Deputy Prov GM and in 1851 he was presented with four silver carved dishes in appreciation of his work in presiding over the Prov Grand Lodge. At his death all Devon lodges were ordered to wear mourning.

Here then is a hall of lasting note which has been literally rescued from its past and reared afresh from the flames. To meet here *is* distinctive for St John's lodge, like other Exeter lodges, has its own opening and closing hymns, its own working, probably through Ancients Grand Lodge influence, and especially its own past memories. When you look at the picture of Richard Bartlett, tyler of this lodge and other Exeter lodges for 40 years, who died in 1775 at the age of 88 you are helped to realise where you are. You are in a hall that is not easy to forget.

The entrance to the temple with Egyptian style pillars.

FAVERSHAM

Willingly to School

OUR VISIT TO Faversham in Kent takes us back to the days of Queen Elizabeth the First. Yet the most attractive and distinctive English building in which the Lodge of Harmony, No 133, at present meets is situated between two other remains of a much older historical past. On the one side you can see the outline of a Norman Abbey founded by King Stephen in 1147 whilst on the other are the remains of a Norman church of still earlier erection. From the church came the Vicars who were among the Masters of the later Elizabethan school whereas it was the Abbey which provided, even before its dissolution, the land and resources for the school's creation.

There was, in fact, a still earlier building on this same site as can be seen from a picture of the Guildhall in a 19th century 'History' but this was put up in 1574 whereas the present school building was put up in 1587. It was actually in 1527 that an indenture between the Abbot of Faversham and Master John Cole, clerk, on the one hand, and the Warden and Fellows of All Souls College, Oxford, on the other, provided for a Free Grammar School within the said monastery for 'the brethren, and novices, and all other children that be disposed to learn the science of grammar . . .'. That was not an altogether unworthy presage of the days when in this same school there would be masonic brethren learning about the seven liberal arts and sciences of which Grammar is one.

It was during a visit to the town by Elizabeth I that the final charter was endorsed to 'erect and establish a Free Grammar School in the town. The Charter was granted on 4 July, 1576'. Whilst the original endowment had been of 317 acres the grant now made was for only 100 acres. One clause of the new Charter at least must have pleased the townsfolk for all the legal charges were waived and the Governors were excused all 'fine or fee by any means to be tendered, paid or done'.

Thus, in 1587, the building which we now see was commenced. The cost was raised by a 'cess' for £30, levied by the Corporation on the town's inhabitants, which thus enabled the purchase of 60 tons of oak timber for the building. It was erected by Nicholas Clerke and Lewis Browne, 'carpenters, inhabitants within the liberty'. An additional and interesting entry in the Wardmote book of 20 February, 30 Eliz. mentions 'the appointment by the Corporation of additional overseers, six in number, who were to make provision of lime, brick, tile, stone, and such like accessories; and for felling timber on the school lands. One of them Abraham Snoode, was to pay the workmen . . .'

The building thus erected consisted of a large schoolroom—the present lodge room—'carried upon well-proportioned and moulded hexagonal oak pillars (of which those on the east side remain) leaving the ground floor free and forming a covered playground for the scholars'. It is again appropriate that this area now forms the dining room for the brethren's recreation. The shallow windows with their leaded lights have moulded frames and mullions and are fixed well above the floor. The whole of the timber framework was fitted together on the ground and marked before erection.

Until 1835, the Corporation, as Governors, held control over the school and its building and were responsible for the administration of its land and revenues but reform of the law led to the appointment of independent trustees who managed affairs until 1879. In that year these 'Governors' resolved to sell the building and its walk in front and this was done by auction for £230, with the walkway going to the Old Pavement Commissioners for £40. The new owner used the lower part of the hall for a store and let off the schoolroom as tenements for one shilling per week each. Indeed he even thought of turning the whole place into a row of cottages.

The Elizabethan 'grammar school' now a masonic hall.

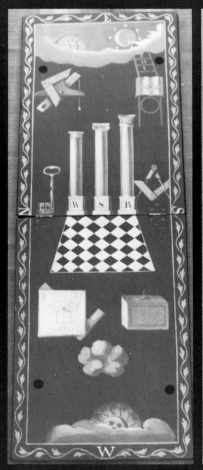

The three ancient and unusual tracing boards.

From this fate the present lovely hall was preserved and by 1887 it had been purchased by the present Masonic lodge whose members began to make good the delapidations of the last seven years. One of their first achievements was to create the refectory area. The old school benches with their poppy-head ends were made into seats and the usher's desk was preserved to become the present Secretary's table. The original doorway into the school or lodge room still survives with the letters NV carved on the left doorpost and M on the right one. These are not special masonic cyphers but refer to Nicholas Upton (Vpton originally) who was Mayor during the time that the building was being erected.

The remains of the old panelling are of special interest since they bear the rude carving and burnt pokerwork which tell of bygone Faversham boys who were first scholars here and then leaders in the town's trade and government. In addition to the overall panelling there are three extra carved pieces which are said to have come 'from an ancient carving in wainscot in the house on the east side of the Abbey Gate'. The panels display the arms of Stephen (with the Archer) and Matilda (with the Knight of the Swan) with a rather unusual arrangement for the central Royal Arms in which the English and French motifs are seen juxtaposed. These panels were given to the lodge, soon after this building was purchased, by the distinguished Kent historian, Francis Frederick Giraud.

The building bears witness to the days of the Window Tax. Some of the front windows were once closed up and are now fully used, whilst in 1907 the fine moulded framing of the south window was discovered, and its space repaired and filled with stained glass to mark the Jubilee of that same Francis Giraud, Town Clerk from 1870–1902. In 1932 another window was opened out on the staircase and even parts of the original lead and tinted glass were found.

The lodge that now fits so naturally into these ancient premises was formed on August 28th 1764 and has duly met in regular assemblies in the same town from then until now. Their volume of the Sacred Law bears the date 1599, thus being a Geneva Bible which was popular before the more familiar Authorised version, and its pages at St. John's Gospel, chapter one, are so soiled that it is difficult even to read the contents. This was a normal and frequent pre-Union custom and one that can be seen in some of the other lodge Bibles figured in this book.

The lodge's 'Rule and Orders' dated 20 May, 1763 are of considerable interest. They are carefully and neatly written and signed 'Laurentio Dermott a Secretis Majoris Coetus'. This shows the lodge to have been one of the 'Antients Grand Lodge' bodies in Kent.

On 1 June, 1859 an entry in lodge records mentions 'Cash paid to Bro Benjamin Thorp, WM of Ashford Lodge for the Pedestal and Tracing Board—the original of the Lodge, £1. 10s.'. This is one of the earliest boards which superseded the painted lodge cloth mentioned in a list of furniture for 1763. The board was either painted by John Cole or from his designs and is the late eighteenth or early nineteenth century work. All the tracing boards here are distinctive and are precious heirlooms of this Lodge of Harmony.

Merely to walk around the temple here is to be struck by the collection of distinctive items that make the Faversham Hall so memorable. Look up at the ceiling with its moulded patterns and notice particularly the four tasselled corners with their pendant knots. Familiar as many masons are with the woven tassels that decorate our carpets in the lodge room it is very striking to see this roof feature. In only two other halls has this been observed and the brethren here are rightly proud of this unusual decoration. The tassel of course has had an interesting history in the Craft and this is not the place to describe that. What I can say, from having sat beneath these carved tassels, is that they even more forcibly reminded me of their heraldic and symbolic allusion—to the widow's cord and thus of our fraternity as those who are widow's sons with HA, or the ends of a measuring line.

Turn now to the Pentacle that also adorns the ceiling, that ancient symbol used in older masonry, and the bright morning star that is here more than just a form of words. At the east end of the room you will see some impressive masonically designed stained glass windows that, lit up from outside at night, give a further tone to this historic meeting place. At the west end of the temple there is a most striking and again unusual 'Chapter' painting which any masonic student would do well to contemplate. What is so memorable is that here, on permanent view, is a

The chapter board over the temple exit.

most revealing scene which stands unashamed whilst only Craft ceremonies are being performed. No mason here is likely to ignore the fact that there is more for him to learn and share than what is seen in the Craft ritual.

It was in 1888 that the records again state "Gifts were received for the Lodge of a pair of globes and stands from WBro Horatio Ward, PPGJW, the R.A. tracing board . . . and brass sconces for the Secretary's desk". The globes, like the R.A. scene just mentioned, are still visible in this lodge and the sconces are adornments to the old Usher's desk which still need polishing. On the west wall there are also two swords formerly belonging to Bro Francis Perkins, a member of the lodge, and these remind the brethren of the two companies of Volunteers formed in 1794 to face the possible threat of Napoleon. These were given in 1890 whilst in the following year a Master Mason's lanthorn was presented by Bro Hooper, which still 'shines like the stars for ever and ever'—at least during lodge meetings.

It is the combination of all these features, together with a small portable R. Arch white pedestal, the large Hiram at the WMs chair and the glorious 'Sun' maul on his desk, which make this not only a memorable masonic hall outwardly and structurally but internally and symbolically. Anyone who has the pleasure of being at a lodge meeting will see something of a Craft that has passed away elsewhere. Here there is a real sense that history is still with us, alive and well. Here we can still learn much.

The east view of the temple. Notice the globes, tassels and the masonic stained glass window.

JERSEY

Jersey after the Jackboot

FOR ANY READER who may be inclined to think of the island of Jersey as principally a tourist resort or offshore finance centre the fact that freemasonry has been actively pursued there for longer than in some parts of the mainland may come as a surprise. Yet this is the case. From at least 1762 onwards there were lodges with travelling warrants working in the island and by the time of the Union in 1813 sixteen of these types of lodge are recorded as having been at work.

In 1765, however, we have the Warrant of the first stationary lodge in the island, Union Lodge No 1. By 1771 the Craft was in a flourishing state as an extract from the diary of one of the King's government officers who lived there clearly shows, and by 1788 there was even a Union Lodge No 2.

In 1812 Lodge Union No 1 was erased but by this time there were three Antients Lodges at work, including the oldest lodge still extant in the island—The Farmers' Lodge, now Yarborough Lodge, No 244. In 1813 the second oldest lodge, The Mechanical Lodge, now the Duke of Normandy Lodge No 245, was warranted, and these two lodges were, incidentally, almost the last lodges to be brought into existence under the Antients Grand Lodge before the Union took place. Their presence, along with 2 Irish stationary lodges in Jersey, seems to account for the use of Antients practices still in local masonic working. One of the latter, Lodge Justice, No 34, Irish Constitution warranted on 3 June, 1813, is known to have worked the Royal Arch ceremony (with Mark as a preliminary), and the Knight Templar degree, all under their Craft Warrant as authorised by the Irish at the time.

Certainly it would seem that from 1765 until the third quarter of the nineteenth century the ritual used in Jersey was the same in all the earlier lodges and showed evidence of some of the older forms. The beginning of a change came with the warranting of the Royal Sussex Lodge, No 491, in 1843 which sought to work in accordance with the changes recommended by the Craft after the Union.

In January 1849 the Samarès Lodge, No 818, was consecrated as a rather select lodge and lasted until 1874, and it was shortly followed by the first French-speaking lodge in the island, Loge la Césarée, No 590. This lodge still continues and is presently the oldest French speaking lodge on the register of the United Grand Lodge of England. In 1861 the Royal Alfred Lodge was founded to provide a masonic gathering place for professional people and retired residents, whilst in 1863 St Aubins Lodge No 958 started in a then more inaccessible part of the island. With yet another newcomer in 1864, the Prince of Wales Lodge No 1003, it can be seen that there were 8 lodges in what was becoming a more sizeable Province and the time for new development and stability had arrived.

It is not surprising to learn therefore that it was in 1864 that the step was taken to house all the lodges in the island in a suitable centre, rather than in dispersed inns and taverns as hitherto. Thus it was that on 25 May, 1864, the present imposing temple in Stopford Road, St Helier, was dedicated. It was planned to be, and happily still is, the centre for all the activities of Freemasonry in Jersey and in the fine tradition of the older masonry that used to be practised in Jersey the other orders of masonry meet here just as do the Craft and Royal Arch. Yet this is to hasten with the story of this hall overmuch. For the present building gains in its value and significance when we realise what it has undergone in the last century.

Certainly the forefathers of present Jersey masons built substantially when they at last sought to create their island 'home'. To gaze today upon the massive

Views of the re-established museum at Stopford Road.

Corinthian pillars that adorn the portico with its two flanking and winding staircases to an elevated entrance door is to see an edifice of public consequence. These same pillars continue down the left hand side of the building and give a sense of restrained opulence to the place. Should anyone wonder what this place might be they are left in no doubt for on the right-hand side of this impressive façade there is a simply decorated gateway with a plain blue door which bears the words 'Masonic Temple'.

When this imposing property was erected there could hardly have been more than 200 brethren in the Island and yet they built this hall which will seat nearly 150 in the Temple and accommodate over 100 for dining. Indeed with such prescience the hall is still adequate for present-day needs even though the number of masons and their lodges has significantly increased. Moreover they provided ample changing rooms, a library and museum, kitchens and space for other orders to operate satisfactorily.

In the museum, by 1939, there was a superb collection of old seals, the famous Vonberg collection of silver and gold jewels, some made by the famous medallist, Thomas Harper. There was the Vacher masonic collection, a number of valuable masonic books and pre-Union certificates, warrants and charts. On the walls of the temple and dining room hung oil portraits of distinguished masons and the silken embroidered banners of the masonic bodies of the Province.

It was to this fine masonic building that disaster suddenly came. On the 1st July, 1940 the Germans landed and occupied this, as others of the Channel Islands. It was considered advisable by local masons to suspend all activities and the hall, save for the dining room and caretaker's living quarters, was locked up. The German authorities were informed of what had happened and approved, saying that nothing would be done to interfere with the contents as long as this arrangement continued.

Whilst other bodies in Jersey were less trusting and buried many of their valuables and treasures the freemasons did not and were soon to discover the difference between the officials of the German Army and the Nazi party. Unfortunately for them they did not safeguard any of their possessions. They were soon to experience the consequences.

On 19th November, 1940 two officers and a private of the Gestapo arrived at the hall without warning and demanded the keys for the temple, chapter room, dining room and library and museum, but left the kitchen and caretaker's rooms free. They sealed the premises before their departure and when in January 1941 a German Army team of 6 officers and a civilian arrived to see whether the hall would be suitable as an army canteen they expressed surprise that the Gestapo had been there and had to admit that they dare not break the seals they found.

A fortnight later German SS troops arrived, made an inventory and took photographs. They were followed four days later by a trained squad of 30 uniformed 'wreckers' specially sent from Berlin and at 8 am the sack of the building began. The entrances to the building were guarded by the Gestapo so that all that could be seen was the removal of loot from within and its being loaded into waiting lorries. In the afternoon another 35 'wreckers' arrived and a number of senior officers visited the hall, presumably to watch what was taking place.

Everything connected with Freemasonry was taken away. Books and small articles were crated but the empty showcases, drawers and wands were smashed and left on the ground. This we know because when the island was finally liberated the remains were still lying about where they had been thrown. The masonic furniture was removed and the smaller pictures either taken away or destroyed. Four of the largest pictures, by the well-known Jersey portrait painter, John St. Helier Lander and presumably too high to be reached, were left hanging on the walls in the temple throughout the war and now, having been renovated, hang again in the temple where they belong. A bonfire was kept going in the grounds with paper and other materials that they did not think worth taking away.

The 'sack' of the premises lasted two days. The Gestapo once more locked the doors and sealed them. Some six packing cases did not go to the harbour and on to Berlin like the rest but were apparently kept by the Commandant at his office as his personal share of the loot. In April, when the Commandants were changed, observers were able to see on the top of the outgoing Commandant's car a rolled up black and white squared carpet. Unfortunately, none of this loot has ever been returned.

Yet that was not all. A few months later an officer and a private again came to the hall. This time they removed most of the domestic furniture such as chairs, tables, cutlery and glass. They took the razor of the caretaker, his toothbrush and his wife's shoes. On complaining to the German Headquarters the personal items were returned with some shirts that had also been removed unnoticed. Other 'visitors' also came in the next two years and finally someone took the only remaining piece of moveable property, the piano. That went in November 1944.

The Master's pedestal positioned in a fine alcove. The twisted pillars are unusual.

The final act of liquidation was when the States of Jersey (the local Parliament) was forced by the German authorities to pass an Act transferring all land and property belonging to the freemasons to themselves. Thus masonry in theory no longer existed.

Throughout the occupation the hall was used as a liquor warehouse. At the Liberation on 8th May, 1945 the temple was found to contain thousands of empty bottles, broken glass and pieces of smashed furniture. Photographs of the time, though taken without flash, show the devastation that was left.

The Nazis are known to have used the material they took for propaganda purposes. An exhibition was staged in Berlin in April 1941 with the object of proving that there was a long-standing conspiracy between Britain and World Jewry. The aim of the plot was world domination and Jersey, a member of the 'Secret Society of World Freemasonry', was shown to be fully involved.

The task of recovery was a far from easy one. There was no lodge furniture, no regalia, no warrants, no lodge minute books—only the bare and dirty shell of the hall we see today. Everything had to be made locally or improvised in a time of national shortage. The aprons of the various degrees were made from old handkerchiefs or other suitable spare material and examples of these are on view at the library and museum of Grand Lodge in London. Substitute warrants were provided in due course and with the eager help of masons from all over the world the hall was restored within a year to something of its former splendour. Then in 1946 there were found in a German archive depot in the American zone of

Looking west with lodge banners proudly displayed.

Germany some cases containing most of the minute books, some of the old records and more than 200 books that now once more grace the library.

The effect on any visitor to this remarkable restoration must be one of surprise that so well-appointed and spacious a building could ever have suffered the indignities that have just been recounted. The entrance hall with its lofty ceiling gives some sense of the general proportions of the building. To rise to the first floor suite of rooms is not to be disappointed. On the left of the principal entrance is the Common or Assembly Room, well supplied with lockers, cupboards and drawers and a double-sided writing desk which avoids the usual crowding known in so many such places elsewhere.

On the top floor of the building is the former Chapter Room now used exclusively for rehearsals or lodges of instruction. In this room (originally purpose-built for Chapter convocations), as elsewhere, the pillars that were seen to adorn the outside of the hall are repeated within and support a fine moulded frieze of red and cream against a background of pale-blue edged walls and vaulted blue ceiling.

The temple itself is three times the size of the former Chapter rooms with walls entirely pale-blue but with the same moulding, frieze and vaulted blue roof. The chairs for the WM, Wardens and 2 flanking PMs in the east are of neo-Gothic style with a distinctly ecclesiastical flavour. They are of oak with plain sturdy legs and well-padded seats. The backs are in the form of an Early English window with three pointed panels, the middle one of which is higher than the rest. These are surmounted by a pointed, decorated top.

The Master's chair, as might be supposed, is rather more elaborate. Flanking the same three but taller rear panels are two slender fluted pillars which are also of the Corinthian order. These are topped by two small globes. Over the central panel with its square and compasses at its head is a carved representation of the VSL in gilt and over this a Sun with the square and compasses yet again.

The chair stands on the top of a podium of one straight and two curved steps and has the WM's pedestal to its right and not, as is common elsewhere, in front. The chair is within a simple apse of pale blue with seven gilt stars painted overhead. The apse is contained within an arch that has a large blue and cream keystone at its summit and beneath the keystone shines a light that is used in the third degree ceremony.

The pedestal for obligations is set in front of the WM but at the foot of the three steps of his podium. It therefore requires that the Master should descend to administer that part of the ceremony. The pedestal here is a simple one of modern design but it bears on its front the circle within 2 parallels which was such a common feature of pre-Union lodges.

At the west end of the chequered carpet is a dark blue covered kneeling stool and flanking it are two spiral mahogany pillars with carved stands and at their head two globes, one terrestrial and the other celestial, held in the semi-circular brass frames that permit the globes easily to revolve. A lovely mahogany display case, holding the hand-painted tracing boards lies at the centre of the carpet.

What particularly strikes a visitor in this temple is the presence of the banners of the Jersey lodges. They add a rich sense of colour and warmth to the room and with the specially delightful Past Master's record boards which cover both the side walls of the temple make this room look especially rich. With the restored pictures in their prominent positions over the door and at the east-end corners the whole effect is impressive. The worst that the jackboot did has been utterly banished.

It is perhaps in the one remaining room upstairs that we are most poignantly made to remember something of the tragedy of those war-time years. As befits a Province that has produced a Lionel Vibert, twice Prestonian lecturer and Secretary of Quatuor Coronati Lodge, great care is taken to see that the library is being well provided for and of the best service to the brethren there. Certainly the presence in the island of another PM of Quatuor Coronati Lodge, Brig A.C.F. Jackson, must help to maintain an interest in the island's treasures and encourage the means of research. Today the visitor will see five large glass-fronted cases full of properly indexed volumes, frames of jewels, a large display case of local and more widespread masonic treasures and a growing series of interesting aprons. As with the rest of the building this is a room with space and light.

Here then is the memorable 'home' of the present 800 masons who live and work in Jersey. It has now more than a century of existence behind it and a part history that few would want to share. Through it all the spirit of the Craft has persisted and any brother or his lady that finds themselves in the island on holiday will be sure to receive a warm welcome from those who are justly proud of this building.

The Chapter temple.

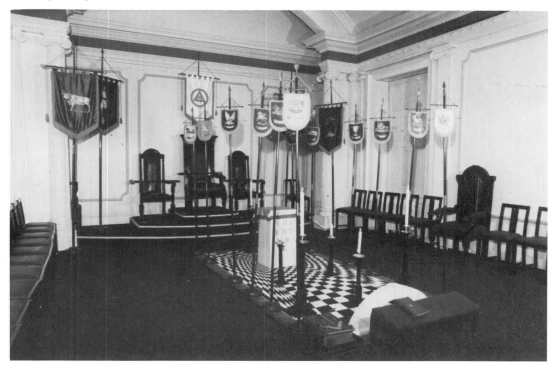

LANGPORT

The Hanging Chapel

TUCKED AWAY IN the Somerset countryside is a tiny masonic meeting place. It stands at one end of the ancient town of Langport and many of us might be hard pushed to know exactly where that is. The town has interesting neighbours like Huish Episcopi and Curry Rivel and is halfway between Bridgwater and Yeovil. It is truly rural.

Where the masons now meet was once a mediaeval chapel, properly called the Chapel of St Mary Eastover. It was built in 1317. It was then used as the Town Hall from 1547 to 1600 and appears to have been in the possession of the Corporation. In 1760 it was taken over as a school and continued as such until 1790 when it became the store used by the militia.

It is known locally as 'the Hanging Chapel' because it straddles or 'hangs over' the carriageway that passes through the archway below. Contrary to one popular myth it has no connection with the Monmouth Rebellion in these parts or the subsequent sentences of hanging imposed by Judge Jeffries in the so-called 'Bloody Assizes'.

The origin of the present arrangement begins with the early 1880s. Up to that time there were still only some 20 or more lodges in Somerset and in spite of being an ancient Borough Langport was one of the places which did not possess its own lodge. Local masons had to travel to Ilminster, Glastonbury or Taunton, and that meant the taking of a horse or wagon over 10 to 14 miles by dirt roads and without lighting. In 1883, however, the minutes of Nyanza Lodge No 1197, meeting at Ilminster record that WBro John Hughes (who lived at Curry Rivel) had unanimous support for an application for a lodge to be formed in this town.

It was thus that the Portcullis Lodge which now meets in this miniature Temple came into existence. It was consecrated as Lodge No 2038 on 24 June, 1884 and though the Wincanton Temperance Fete was celebrated on the same day it does not seem to have unduly affected the attendance! The lodge began by meeting in the Langport Arms Hotel (where its Festive Board is still held) and continued thus for the next seven years.

The possibility of building a new masonic hall was then considered but even with the generous offer of the first £100 from an anonymous brother the matter was not proceeded with. This may well have been because there was already wind of the chance to use the 'Hanging Chapel' and since the normal attendances at the lodge were about 12 brethren (with 16 to 24 on special evenings) use of the chapel as a lodge room seemed ideal. In June 1891 a 12 year lease was signed at a rent of

The temple interior with prominent pillars.

The Hanging Chapel at Langport is an unlikely setting for a Masonic hall.

£4 per annum and the necessary alterations were put in hand. The cost of these was £60 and the first meeting took place in November of that same year.

The members of the Portcullis Lodge are currently tenants of the Langport Parish Council who took over from the former owners, the Langport Town Trust. Due to the age of the building the 1960s saw the need for considerable repairs and after these had been carried out the Provincial Grand Master re-dedicated the building in 1971.

The temple is approached by a flight of seven steps on the right of the archway as you come from the town centre. A simple wooden door bearing the masonic square and compasses tells any passer-by the purpose of the premises above. You then mount a further five steps within the arch's retaining wall and three to enter a simple ante-room which runs the whole length of the side of the chapel or temple. A curtain at one end of the ante-room serves to form the tyler's preparation area for candidates and the rest is occupied with a signature table, pegs for the officers' jewels, and a notice board for local use. Opposite the small signing table is a flight of stairs which leads into the temple itself. The intervening door has a fine brass knocker, a strong iron handle and a sliding peep-hole. You enter the chapel beside the Junior Warden's pedestal.

The room you enter is only 25 ft by 15 ft but apart from the obvious difficulty of finding enough seating for today's much larger attendances it is a perfectly formed temple. Two fine Corinthian style wooden pillars with chapiters and two celestial and terrestrial globes immediately strike you on entering as they stand in the centre of the carpet but nearer to the Senior Warden, with a red kneeling stool between them and his pedestal. It is interesting to note how this lodge, which could so properly decide to remove the pillars because of space (as some other temples in this book have done), steadfastly continues to insist on their presence. With their solid wood bases, and set in a room that had plain but well-maintained wood panelling around its four sides, there is a sense of warmth and dignity in this otherwise tiny room.

The upper parts of the walls are tastefully colourwashed in pale blue and this is continued on the two ends of the round vaulted ceiling whilst the canopy itself is covered with a delicate array of stars. This, at least, gives a much greater sense of space and light to what could otherwise be a cramped and confined area.

There are two hamstone windows in the north side of the lodge room which were, for many years, blocked up. In 1915 these were exposed and it was found that the stonework was still complete and undamaged. Stained glass was inserted by the brethren who thus gave the chapel-temple something of its original appearance. Each window consisted of two lights, the first containing a representation of the Virgin Mary to whom the chapel was first dedicated—and who was, of course, one of the original patrons of the masons craft—and in the other light they placed a representation of the Angel Gabriel.

The second window bore a likeness of King Alfred who was closely associated with this region, whilst he was flanked by Lady Margaret, Countess of Richmond and Derby, mother of Henry VII, a notable landowner locally and whose portcullis emblem is not only incorporated in the Borough's coat of arms but has also given the symbol and name to the lodge that meets here.

The principal chairs together with their splendid pedestals reflect nineteenth century masonic work at its best. They are decorated with the appropriate emblems and add a true sense of dignity to the room. Other heirlooms of the lodge are the "copper jug" which holds loose change given at the festival board for charity, a set of engraved, short but wide mouthed firing glasses and a ram's horn snuff mill. There is also a pair of turned wooden candlesticks, made from the trunk of an ancient tree (believed to be a thorn and about 2000 years old) which was dug up in Sedgemoor by WBro William Lampert and then turned by his own hand.

It only remains to quote from the 1984 Centenary history to remind visitors that the Portcullis motif seen here on the lodge banner reflects the same motif carved in the bench ends in the Parish Church just a few yards away towards the town centre.

A Portcullis particularly lends itself to Masonic interpretation . . . The iron-shod ends of the *three* centre beams each show two barbs, or points: on the outside beams only one is disclosed: whilst the Chains, of course, exhibit no points at all . . .

An examination of the Chains on either side reveals that between the shackle pin at the top and the holding ring at the bottom there are 15 links. These have an allusion to those two groups of FCs. The whole is encompassed by a circle, the centre of which is the centre bolt, a five pointed star. This star raises in our minds the 5 points of fellowship. It marks that point from which . . . a Master Mason cannot err. . . .

Here then is yet another memorable masonic hall. Not large and not easily found. Indeed its future is already in the balance. I count it a delight to have seen it still as a place of masonic work. I hope it hangs on for many years yet.

Notice the door and the stone multioned window between the pillars.

LEWES

The Old Hall at Lewes

THE SOUTH SAXON Lodge No 311, which nowadays meets in and owns the Freemasons Hall in the High Street at Lewes, Sussex, began its life in the Star Inn in that town in 1796. Within a year 'the many unpleasant inconveniences frequently arising to them (the members), by the lodge· room being sometimes unavoidably engaged and taken up by the Landlord for the accommodation of other people on the regular lodge nights', it was proposed to erect for the Bretheren (*sic*) of this lodge a proper commodious place to assemble in. A tablet which tells of the laying of the foundation stone of this first hall by Major-General Hulse is still preserved in the wall of the cellar, having been laid on 19 April, 1797. It was at last occupied on October 5th.

During the next twenty years this ancient lodge was to act as the Provincial Grand Lodge from time to time and the two jewels used during that period are also retained in the premises at present occupied. They are, significantly, those of the PGM and the Provincial Tyler. A meeting of the Provincial Grand Lodge was held first in 1801 in the 'Hall of the SOUTH SAXONS' but by 1817 the lodge had transferred to 'their hall in the eastern tower of Lewes Castle' and the present building was let for other purposes. It was at this castle site that the ceremonies of the Craft were performed for the next 40 years.

In 1867 the minutes of the lodge suggest the formation of a committee to 'ascertain the price at which the premises now occupied by the Lodge can be purchased and to report on . . . the cost of enlarging the present room, and employ an architect for that purpose if necessary'. The committee reported that it was worth 'quite £200'. That was in March and by July the sale had been completed and not only the hall but an adjoining property too had become available. Alterations to the sum of £300 were also approved.

On 21 October, the foundation stone of the present 'New Freemasons Hall' was laid, following which ceremony no less than 150 persons 'sat down to a most recherché Banquet supplied in Brother Geer's best style, in the Corn Exchange'. A year later the Building Committee was empowered to 'lay out an additional £50 on the front of the Hall'—the one we see today. Thus was created the first purpose-built hall for the Craft in the Province of Sussex. It will therefore be no surprise to learn that the members of the South Saxon Lodge are justly proud of it. Its erection formed a landmark in the progress of Sussex Masonry.

The façade of the building may at first sight seem unremarkable. Almost flush on to what is a very busy street during the day, and being but one more frontage amongst all the other properties in the upper High Street, one needs to pause across the road and take time to appreciate the design. It is made of stone, yellow and red brick and yet obvious care has been taken to convey to the initiated something of what goes on behind the shuttered or darkened windows.

The entrance porch is flanked by two stone pillars carrying a Gothic arch of which there is a most evident keystone, specially marked. This arch is covered moreover by two sides of an equilateral triangle, as if Deacons' wands were placed in position. The doorway moreover is painted blue.

To the right of the entrance is a row of three identical windows with another, shallower arch of red brick uniting them. The sills and pediments of the windows are of stone and above the windows are floral designs that seem to represent an acacia plant. Between this arch and the tops of the windows are red and yellow alternate squares which suggest perfect ashlars.

Two parallel and horizontal lines of red brick now carry the eye to the first floor and to the two much larger windows that are behind the east end of the upstairs temple. One of these windows is placed exactly over the apex of the 'wands' that cover the entrance whilst the other window is over the central part of the three lower windows. The balance and harmony are very striking and this is further enhanced by a further arch of yellow and red brick that links the similar smaller arches over these upper casements. But what cannot be avoided is the one exceptional introduction of blue bricks to make a band of red and blue design which perfectly reproduces the edge of the lodge carpet in the Royal Arch tints. With a regular stone between the upper windows describing the hall's erection the whole front of this hall is complete.

You enter the building to find a foyer where coats may be hung and on the right of this a door leading into a downstairs ante-room filled with fascinating and some recherché objects. A cupboard contains some pots of older use in the lodge, especially one marked with the lodge's name and of no little use when the lavatory facilities were not what they are today. There are jugs for ale of fine design, a small coffin lid once used in ceremonies, the original foundation stone, and a most intriguing iron plate showing Faith and Hope, the Sun, Moon and seven stars and many other well-known lodge jewels. It is set within the indented border of a typical carpet design and no-one as yet knows for what purpose it was made or when it became simply a wall decoration. (Compare the one in the Brighton hall.) The foundation stone of the present building is near the door to the stairs.

As with so many older lodges and their halls there are examples here of French prisoner of war jewels, made from scraps of metal but exquisite in workmanship. There are also a fine picture of William IV in a blue frock coat and with regalia, a certificate issued in Nova Scotia, and a Volume of the Sacred Law, presented by the Charter Master, which opens most naturally at the first chapter of John. One interesting picture here shows the original building on the site, and the showcase of jewels contains some less usual items.

From the corner of the room opposite to the entrance door the brethren ascend a winding staircase of two flights to reach a small area used as both the signing and preparation area by the tyler. This compact space is also filled with some priceless items of local masonic interest. There is the sombre flag that was flown from the Castle wall when the lodge met—it bears a skull and crossbones on a black background. Here too are kept the somewhat different chapter carpet and the 15 metal Royal Arch banners which are amongst the oldest in any English hall today.

It is from here that you pass through a door with two very unusual 'knocking boards' into the temple itself. You are immediately aware of its simple dignity. The room gives the impression of being a double cube with the upper half plain and plastered. The lodge at ground level is a pleasing arrangement of time-honoured items.

The feature that particularly strikes many visitors (and as one sees also at Taunton) is the array of masonic implements always laid out in the centre of the floorcloth, which is black and white throughout. On a Turkey red carpet and starting from east to west are the rough and smooth ashlars, a wooden tripod which stands on the apex of wooden compasses and the points where that pair of compasses crosses the segment of a circle. The perfect square stone that is suspended from the tripod by a miniature lewis is decorated and painted. Beneath it is a stone tile with many masonic emblems and this is the plate held by the Junior

Looking east with columns beside Master's pedestal. Notice the large JW's pedestal and the floor display.

The ancient 'tile'

The old Mark tracing board.

Left: *The old South Saxon banner.* Below left: *Second degree tracing board.* Below: *The floor display.*

Deacon at the north east corner. Next come a heavy maul, a large brass G and a larger than usual poignard, alongside the chisel, gavel, skirret and pencil. Finally, at the west end of the lay-out there is a miniature pedestal, open VSL with a ladder rising from it and having 15 or more rungs, a pair of dividers, and finally a fully-sized level, plumbline and square. Interestingly there is also an unusual 24 " rule and one wonders if this, like the dividers, was meant to provide the same symbolic significance. All these items are mentioned in the lodge's inventory of 1823 though their spelling then is of interest—"Ashlar, Plum rule, Skillet and line, three Hyrams and Sett Gin Poles'.

These items are sometimes referred to by the PMs here as the 'Tracing Board'. The rough and perfect ashlars are placed at the NE and SE corners of the display, the working tools are grouped according to the degrees (first degree tools and poignard in the north, for example) and the JD adjusts the compasses there in time with the IPM in the east. The old working tools are the ones presented and explained to a new WM at Installation.

Also mentioned then is "1 very Elegant Mahgy Chair & Stand" together with three pedestals and candlesticks (viz Ionic, Doric & Corinthian). The furniture lives up to its reputation. The W. Master's chair has a tall back with the semblance of two 'pillar' panels at its sides surmounted with a small globe each and a gold plated winged eagle between them. The chair itself sits within a black and gold painted canopy of classical design though once again the form is of a rounded arch with a small keystone, underneath a more formal pointed arch. The pedestals are all uniform being a simple wooden shaft between four carved pillars at each corner—their form being that appropriate to the officer who sits at them. The candlesticks are similarly carved and the columns at the Wardens' places are distinguished by having chequered and stepped bases. There was also a Master's column now 'renovated' and placed in the downstairs display case. On the Secretary's table are two modest but fine silver candlesticks that are always lit during meetings, whilst behind the table and above the dado which runs around the whole room there is a most elegant showcase with its own candleholders and containing the original and Provincial Grand Lodge warrants of No 311.

The three lodge tracing boards are of fine quality being mentioned in the Inventory of 1852 as "with cord and tassels". The dress of the Deacons on the second degree board suggest their early Victorian provenance and the first degree board is unusual in not having any figures on the Jacob's ladder and portraying a smooth ashlar remarkably like the one suspended from the tripod in the centre of the lodge floor. The original second degree tracing board fell into the fire in the 1970s and was sent to London for repair. The lodge has likewise a beautifully framed Old Mark tracing board.

It is in the same inventory that we read of '1 Organ fixd in Wall said to have been Queen Elizabeth and Stool for Organist'. Certainly this instrument, even if not now proved to be quite so old, adds yet more to the overall atmosphere as does the old De Warenne banner that is framed above it.

One item of the lodge's possessions remains to be noted. It is a copy of the picture by A. Archer RA which depicts 'The visit of their most Gracious Majesties William IV and Queen Adelaide to the Ancient Borough of Lewes on the 22nd October, 1830'. In the picture can be seen many members of the lodge attired in masonic clothing, their Craft and RA banners. The minutes of 22 October that year for a Lodge of Emergency state: ' . . . on her Majesty's ascending the heights of the Western Tower, the Brethren were assembled on the leads of their Lodge and saluted the Queen with loyal and enthusiastic cheers . . . which her Majesty was pleased to acknowledge by bowing repeatedly to the Brethren in the most affable and condescending manner'. There can be little doubt that the present members of the South Saxon Lodge would be equally proud to salute their Sovereign today from the roof of this distinguished and fascinating building.

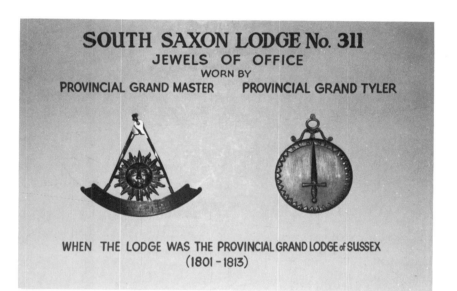

SOUTH SAXON LODGE No. 311
JEWELS OF OFFICE
WORN BY
PROVINCIAL GRAND MASTER   PROVINCIAL GRAND TYLER

WHEN THE LODGE WAS THE PROVINCIAL GRAND LODGE of SUSSEX
(1801 - 1813)

LISKEARD

A Cornerstone in Cornwall

IN 1845 THE life of the town of Liskeard reflected many of the aspects of a new and developing Cornwall. The mines at Caradon and in the surrounding district were approaching the peak of their productivity and providing employment for several thousand men and women. Part of the Caradon railway linking the mines with the Liskeard and Looe canal had just been completed. A coach passed through the town on its regular journey from Truro to Torpoint. The tradesmen living over their shops worked from 10 to 12 hours every day and there were cattle markets and fairs held on the Parade. The horse was the most speedy form of transport still, there were no motor cars and no electricity. Liskeard was just beginning to experience prosperity.

It was in this town that on 27 January a petition was submited to the Earl of Zetland to form a Lodge of St Martin, so named after the local Parish Church. It was to meet at the Fountain Inn in the town and its first senior officers, all solicitors, bore names and associations that are in themselves intriguing.

The first Master was to be Edward Lyne who had been WM of Lodge 'One and All' in 1842: and the SW was no less than Bro Simon Peter: and the JW was to be Bro Samuel Binney Serjeant. Bro Henry Grylls, the Provincial Grand Chaplain, signed the petition but apparently never became a member. What is even more interesting is that the lodge met seven times before it was actually consecrated and at these meetings 7 men were initiated whilst six became joining members and one serving brother was admitted. When it came to the Consecration day on 19 August it is good to note that "the Police seemed not to be needed, so correctly did everyone appear to act, nor did we hear of a single accident or unpleasantness."

It is further worth noting that before the constituting of the lodge at its meeting room there was a service in the Parish Church at which 3 clergy took part in addition to the Provincial Grand Chaplain who preached on *Romans* chapter 1, verse 20. Following the consecration proper there was a banquet 'with all the dainties procurable' and after the cloth had been removed the Ladies entered the room and joined in the toasts!

In 1850 the lodge removed from the Fountain Inn to a room of Bro Lyne's office in Church Street (the rental being £5 pa). This must have caused some upset for within a matter of months it moved again to the London Inn where the Public Hall now stands. It stayed there for the next 21 years.

On 13 October, 1868, a Lodge of Emergency was held to decide on whether a masonic hall should be erected and a committee was appointed to see if a site and funds could be procured. It was not until three years later that they were able to act

Liskeard Masonic Hall in the town square.

when it became known that the Devon and Cornwall Bank (now Lloyds) was prepared to sell a site next to their premises. The price asked for was £150! By a majority of 15 to 2 it was agreed in lodge that £50 be granted from the funds and that the members should raise the remainder. The response to the appeal for the sum required was so successful that on 17 August, 1872, the brethren, in full craft clothing, and headed by the band of the Liskeard Volunteer Corps, processed to the site. In the presence of hundreds of ordinary spectators the Deputy Provincial Grand Master laid the foundation stone with full masonic ceremonial.

The first meeting was held on December 30th even though the ceremony of dedication did not occur until 6 August, 1873. This was the first official act of the new PGM, the Rt Hon the Earl of Mount Edgcumbe, and following this ceremony a procession was formed in which the Mayor, attended by his mace-bearers, proceeded to Wadham House where a bazaar in aid of the building fund was opened.

The amount spent on land, building, decoration and legal expenses came to

The substantial pillars and globes are a feature of the hall together with the tracing boards behind the Senior Warden's place.

£1171. The furniture that was required cost £64 and of this the lodge funds had only to provide £11 after generous gifts by the members. The mortgage for the building was finally discharged to coincide with the 50th anniversary of the St Martin's Lodge foundation.

Today we see a typically Victorian, specially designed Masonic Hall with the same furnishings that first graced the meetings of those early Liskeard masons. The façade of local stone, with its dog-tooth frieze at the level of the first storey floor, and its impressive row of four round-headed, pilastered and arched stained glass windows above, gives the building an early mediaeval appearance and accords well with the large and ancient square at the side of which it stands. The ground floor has a pair of linked windows with shallow-arched heads and keystones standing prominently at the centre of each. To their left is the slender doorway, flanked by two pillars leading to the triangular shaped portico, and itself at the top of three steps. At the very top of the façade and just beneath the Cornish slate roof runs a band of masonic motifs—18 crossed square and compasses.

The east view of the temple with masonic symbols incorporated in the window. The round backed chairs have officers' emblems.

The downstairs accommodation is today let out to a local professional firm in order to raise some income to assist with the hall's upkeep and one thus passes to the rear staircase which leads to the masonic temple and dining room above. In 1899, after some four years of discussion, it was decided to change the arrangement of the rooms upstairs by incorporating an ante-room at the head of the stairs (to the left) into the then smaller temple. This meant that the width of the lodge room grew from a previous 17 ft 6 in to 25 ft and provided the almost square appearance that we observe today.

What immediately strikes the visitor is the sense of unity in the furnishings and the fact that we have here a lodge room that has now been used continuously for over a century in almost exactly the same fashion as we can view it. We are told by the lodge historian that in re-decoration in 1902 there was a triple curtain of the three special masonic colours—blue, crimson & purple—across the east end but that was subsequently removed. The present arrangement is no less striking, especially when the temple is visited in daylight for behind the serried rank of stout, carved oak chairs that flank the taller, spiralled pillar-back chair of the Master we have the benefit of the four stained glass windows which are representations of four acts of mercy and charity based on the life of St. Martin. In each of these windows is a mass of masonic symbolism and allusion, the latter especially related to the brother in whose memory each of the windows was given.

Behind the Master's chair there stands the banner of the lodge, an excellent and so far well-preserved representation of St Martin dividing his cloak with the leper, albeit the clothing of St Martin is several centuries later in style than the original story would warrant. On the rich red-papered wall space between the windows is a display case showing some of the masonic medals and collarettes of several masonic degrees.

Before central heating was installed in 1933 the room was heated by two open fires and the white marble surrounds of these, adorned with a central panel of the square and compasses, and two corner circles enclosing the Seal of Solomon, are still prominent in the décor. It is their presence which adds a sense of continuity to the layout. It is on the mantelpieces of these fireplaces that we find two noticeable items—one, a fine naval officer's sword which was once used by the tyler; and the other, a most unusually shaped ballot box of oak. Standing on a square base in which there is a drawer for the black and white balls the voting box has a circular rimmed base, a slender, round column and then a graceful globe-shaped receptacle into which has been cut an oval aperture into which the hand can be inserted to place the vote unseen. It is at once a delicate piece of lodge furniture and a most reliable guide to true balloting.

The most impressive part of the lodge room yet remains to be described. It is in the centre of the temple and consists of a beautifully inlaid tiled mosaic area about 12 ft by 6 ft with a border of alternate and indented triangles. This covers the exact centre of the floorspace. It is flanked at the west end of the tiling with two brown marble columns, standing some ten feet high with carved chapiters and one of the two appropriate globes resting thereon. They are, of course, hollow and are actually made of wood! Beside the black square base of the left hand pillar, facing east and on its eastward front, there stands the usual tripod on its wooden base and with a plain white smooth ashlar suspended from the apex. Between the two pillars lies a long, red coloured kneeling stool.

The overall intimacy of this lodge room and the sense of historical pride that so obviously attends it is also confirmed by one extract from the lodge history. We read there that at some early installations the placing of the Worshipful Master in the Chair was immediately followed by the lodge being called off, not merely for a few moments, but for the serving of a whole dinner in the lodge room. When the banquet was completed labour would be resumed, presumably still at the table, the business was concluded and the lodge closed (cf. the old practice in Ludlow, Vol II). It is also recorded that in 1892 when the toast to 'Past Masters, Treasurer and Secretary' was proposed ALL the PMs in turn responded! As we look round what was then a room with its cheery coal fires and fine oak furnishing with heavy curtains it can be well imagined that time mattered little and festivity banned all sense of protracted proceedings. Today there is an adequate dining room and kitchen beyond the stairs but as I retraced my steps and descended to the square of this typical Cornish town I could only reflect that this was but one corner of the larger tapestry of masonry that Cornwall can provide. It was that thought which made this sample of it so memorable. I left St Martin's Hall with the distant sound of that 1892 Installation still vividly in my mind—'In the course of the evening capital songs and recitations were given by the WM and Bros Stanton, Williams, Henwood, Rawlings, Hicks, Venning, Hallett, White, Foddy, Ayres, Smith, Luget . . .

NEWPORT

At the Heart of an Island

NEWPORT LIES ALMOST at the centre of the Isle of Wight. Until a century or so ago it was a thriving haven for smaller sea-going vessels and its quays are still visible to this day even if the business which was once done on them is no more. With that trade came a prosperous class of merchants and traders and not a few of those same men became the proud founders and supporters of Albany Lodge which was founded in 1801. The island was also of some considerable military importance during this Napoleonic period and large numbers of soldiers were stationed there. Indeed the moving spirit behind the founding of Albany was a retired NCO and the first WM was a serving soldier. There was already another lodge called 'Hiram' but unlike Albany, which has persisted to the present, the earlier lodge ceased to meet in 1828.

The Albany Lodge first met at an Inn called the 'Castle and Banner' on Hunny Hill but changed its lodging in 1806 and then met in various places until 1848 when the present Masonic Hall was built specifically as a permanent meeting place. The hall was subsequently improved and this event is recorded on the front of the present hall where, in a series of five panels over the moulded course that runs above the ground floor windows, there is the following:

A.D.1892   Aude   Vide   Tace   A.L.5892

The hall which bears this message on its façade lies itself at the heart of the town and stands naturally and distinctively amongst surrounding two-storied Regency town houses. Whilst they are tiled and plastered the hall is made almost entirely of mellow red brick with a no less imposing three-columned brick chimney stack surmounting the front like a crown.

The façade shows two floors and each of substantial height. On the ground floor there is a blue painted door to the left with the three plain and round-arched windows of the dining room to its right.

Between the first and second windows the outside wall bears a circular motif surrounded by keystones and showing at its centre an ancient ship with its canvas unfurled and upon the sea—the heraldic emblem of the town. In the centre of the first floor row of four rectangle windows the purpose of the hall is more specially emphasised. Within an oblong frame is a circle touching the two upright parallels, and within this circle the Seal of Solomon (two interlaced triangles) with another smaller triangle at the heart of the emblem. Flanking the windows there are six simulated pillars of brick with elaborately decorated chapiters and moulded bases.

Opposite: *The richly decorated canopy above the Master's pedestal and the archstones beside it are unusual.*

Masonic Hall, Newport, Isle of Wight with masonic inscription and decoration.

An indented frieze of brick runs around the base of the gently pitched/tile roof. The whole effect is dignified and gracious.

From the functional entrance hall one turns right into the dining room that lies behind the ground floor windows. This room at once announces the historical interest one associates with this hall for its furnishings and mementoes are a visual record of the earliest days of the Albany Lodge. The Worshipful Master's chair is a replica of a Jersey Estates Council chair, whilst the Past Master's chair and a set of other chairs to match are marked 176 and have appropriate masonic emblems carved neatly into their rounded spindle backs. The overall effect is one of the earlier tavern settings in which these chairs must have been used.

Hanging on the walls are 2 unusual mineral bottle trays with the indentations to permit the old glass containers to be handed round at table. These take their place amongst a complete set of rummer glasses of the period 1832–1863 and all are engraved 'Albany Lodge 176'. There are also some silver-plated pipe lighters in the shape of a bell and dated 1890. All these items help to form some idea of the previous life of the brethren who met in this room and one more item still helps to maintain that older connection.

On the mantelpiece in this room there stands an ancient clock. The clock was installed in the Castle and Banner Inn in the earlier half of the 19th Century and there it stayed until the inn was burned down between 1840 and 1850. It was then rescued and taken across the road to the 'House of Industry' (or Workhouse) and there it remained until 1901 when it was handed over to the brethren of Albany Lodge on their supplying another timepiece to serve in its place. The clock bears the name of Robert Trattle, Newport and is distinguished also by having an Hermetic picture on its front.

The other fascinating items from about the same date are a front door letter box, an unusual front door lock and a very different kind of doorkey. A description of these items explains the origin of the term 'keyhole'.

The other items in this lofty room are the most attractive old banners that have been preserved in stout glass frames. In order of age they are as follows:

An eighteenth century banner showing the compass in the FC position, with a Pentagram at the centre enclosing a large G.
A Banner of the Peace and Concord chapter founded here in 1810.
The banner of the Provincial Grand Master of the Isle of Wight 1812 when it formed a separate masonic area, together with a photograph of Sir Leonard Holmes, MP, the PGM.
A Mark Banner of 1848, well before the foundling of the present Mark Grand Lodge, and marked AL 5777.

It can be imagined that with this wealth of history around them the brethren dining in this room are naturally proud of their meeting place. As they raise their eyes, as well as their glasses, they have yet one more pleasing sight. Near the ceiling are three Chippendale cornices of delightful design. They were placed there after having been taken down from Appledurcombe House, the residence of the Earl of Scarborough, Provincial Grand Master in 1826.

Also on the ground floor is a modest robing room with yet another pentagram in stained glass on the entrance door. Here too are distinctive signs of an earlier masonry on the island. There is an example of the regalia worn in the Isle of Wight before 1869 and also a craft apron in red worn by Minden Lodge No 63 which met here in 1848 in order to start the Albany Mark Lodge of which we have already seen a banner in the dining room. This intimation of pre-Mark Grand Lodge Masonry is but one of several others that were to come to light upstairs. On the way up there we encounter on the stairs a coloured print with many intriguing illustrations, named as KST and in the style of a multi-degree chart.

At the top of the stairs we move into a spacious tyler's room with its array of masonic treasures. To carry on the Mark connection here we find a list of Mark members in 1848 with all their marks set out in a unique frame. There is also a drawing of a pre-1857 Mark keystone and 2 old Mark jewels, one still used today and the other a distinctive one of pre-Mark Grand Lodge vintage. A Mark 'Time Immemorial' certificate in cypher completes this special collection.

Turning to the Craft there is a clearance certificate for Lodge 200 at the Castle and Banner Inn in 1805 and, still earlier, a small chart of 1802 produced by a Bro Cole. In the Royal Arch we see a similar chart displaying the three Principals, whilst in another corner is another clearance certificate from the Grand Superintendent in Cornwall of 1868. It was in this room that the brethren laid out for me the chapter carpet and the delicate, pillared arch with its moveable keystones so that I might see how Albany Chapter have always performed their ceremony. This rather more graceful 'arch' was one that appears in lodge rooms further to the west of England but this was the first time that I saw it being used on the floor of a Royal Arch chapter. Elsewhere they seem to stay on or behind the Secretary's table.

Perhaps the most intriguing item of an extra-mural kind in the room is a public notice that reads as follows:

CRICKET
will be played
On Monday the 16th of August, 1819
BY
Eleven Gentlemen
AGAINST NEWPORT
on
Mr. STEPHEN'S GROUND, Castle and Banner
near Newport.

WICKETS to be PITCHED at TEN O'CLOCK

A good Ordinary will be provided

Whether or not this notice in the tyler's room reassures any present candidate that what is to happen in the adjacent lodge room will at least be fair play I do not know. What certainly reminded me that the tyler of old was more than just a preparer of candidates was the presence of a plate-warmer. At least the candidate could be certain that this helpful brother was mindful of our later creature comforts.

Before moving into the adjacent temple there was one more item to catch the eye especially as it concerned a no less remarkable and memorable hall in the north of England (see Vol III of this series). It was a Knight Templar Preceptory Certificate of 1813 issued from Minerva Hall, Kingston upon Hull. It is headed

> In the Name of the Father, Son, and
> Holy Ghost.   AMEN.

and bears the strips of red, blue and white ribbon which apparently seal its authenticity. Knowing as we do the antiquity of the Encampment at Kingston upon Hull this document has especial interest for any in that order but what makes it all the more interesting is that here, at the other end of the country, we have the formal recognition of members of that order and its obvious spread across the whole length of England.

To pass into the temple is to discover yet more masonic features of a distinctive kind. The room is wide and lofty, a double cube in dimension, and displays many striking marks.

The Master's chair is set within a canopy and is flanked by a whole set of chairs made for and numbered 176. The Director of Ceremonies' chair has its own distinctive emblem. In addition to the later Victorian seats there are some simpler but striking 176 chairs with sharp, triangular-shaped backs. The Master's pedestal has a false front which can be removed to reveal a skull and crossbones

A bottle dish belonging to Lodge 176.

The Royal Arch model which stands about 14 inches in height.

transparency that is lit up at the appropriate moment of a ceremony. What is bound to intrigue the inquisitive visitor here, however, is that on the pedestal lies a perfectly normal looking VSL which bears on its spine the words 'Holy Bible'. If you open it up you will be surprised, as were some of the local brethren, to discover that it only contains the books of the Old Testament, finishing at the book of the prophet, Malachi. It is certainly one of only two so far as any of the halls in this present collection are concerned. (See Exeter p.56) Moreover, though the volume is now opened mostly at the book of Chronicles it is quite obvious from the very soiled pages that it was customary once to open the VSL at the book of Ruth, as is still the custom in Bristol and some other centres.

Other objects of peculiar remark stand on the shelf above the old fireplace behind the Secretary's table in the north. These include two old Wardens' staves as well as one that bears the emblem of the Treasurer. They are about 2 ft 6 in in length but have not been in use in living memory. Besides them are two large triangular medallions each containing a picture of some part of the Chapter story, whilst close by is a frame for setting out the candles in the middle of the lodge board, or later carpet.

Yet the most remarkable feature of this richly stocked lodge room is the abundance of framed items that fill its walls. A mere list can only begin to whet the appetite of the determined enquirer but it is hoped that it will begin to give some idea of the wealth of masonic information that is stored in this island hall.

An old Royal Arch tracing board.

1. A framed pre-Union Floorcloth which looks more like a chart than a mere covering or pavement.
2. The banner of the Albany Lodge from 1832–63, showing a figure with the words *Tout Ung Durant Ma Vie* and a brass trowel at the base.
3. The Isle of Wight banner of the PGM, Thomas Flemming, in 1852.
4. A large tracing board of the Chapter showing a circular base to the altar and with the ensigns in their correct positions, also in a circle.
5. An old Chapter tracing board showing the Vault.
6. The picture of a Chapter apron of 1811.
7. An old Royal Arch banner ITNOT-GA-OTU surrounding the Royal Arch symbol.
8. A Masonic chart by Finch.
9. Two Mark cypher lists of members.
10. A Minden Lodge No 63 Keystone marked 20 Regt and showing also the reverse.
11. 6 Mark Keystones forming a broken arch with a pedestal in the centre.
12. A Mark emblematical charter in cypher, dated 1854.
13. An old Mark tracing board.

As can be seen from this mere catalogue we have here a very remarkable collection at the heart of this island. It is a collection of which the local brethren can be justly proud. Perhaps the last feature of their hall to be mentioned is one about which they should think again.

On the West wall of the temple there hang the four principal banners of the Royal Arch. Like the banners that bear the emblems of the 12 tribes they are old and special, especially as the tribal banners are still of the original metal style. At the centre of the four main banners is a very old yellow banner that stands immediately over the Principal Sojourner's chair. On being asked what was the script of the word written upon it no-one seemed to know. What then became evident was that the banner had once been repaired and the repairer had inverted the cloth. What could not be read was the Tetragrammaton upside down. It is not really to the honour of the Royal Arch companions that this should continue but such is the devotion of the brethren to their possessions that they are reluctant to disturb any of their heirlooms, Perhaps this is where one exception could be made.

POOLE

The Pleasure of Old Poole

IF YOU EXPLORE the seaward end of this old Dorset seaport you will still be able to imagine what this town was like in the early years of the nineteenth century. The solid but pleasant lines of the Town Hall of the day, with its specially graceful double curved stairways leading to the four-pillared portico at first floor level, and that portico standing above a white rusticated stone doorway with fine oak doors and wide fanlight, suggest the prosperity and elegance of that period in this town's history. To walk around the square and lanes that still enclose the nearby parish church of St James gives the same impression though one can soon be aware of the modern, bustling shopping area which most tourists probably recall.

It is in this older area of Poole and within 200 yards of the old Town Hall that there stands a four square Georgian town house. It has two rows of 4 identical sash windows with their 12 panes apiece, all with white sills and frames set in the rich dark red brick that is used in so many of the buildings hereabout. To the right of this solid frontage there stands the entrance. By three wide stone steps one mounts to a plain, panelled white door bearing the number 4. Beside the door are two elongated windows with their own white sills whilst above the door is a brick coping with a plain white keystone. Yet beneath the delicate balustrade that surmounts the entrance and finishes it off at first floor level there is the most intriguing feature of all. Jutting out from the top of the keystone and hanging over the steps is a wrought copper lantern. Its sides are made of white opaque glass and upon them are inscribed the words

LODGE
AMITY

so that no passerby can be in any doubt as to the purpose for which this building is now used.

The house was in fact built as the home of one of those Georgian merchants whose prosperity grew with the trade that flowed through eighteenth and early nineteenth century Poole. Whilst the house was occupied by the families that owned it the Amity Lodge No 137 was renting accommodation in a number of hostelries in the immediate vicinity—the Lion and Lamb, the Antelope, the new Antelope. It continued this wandering existence from 1765 to 1880 when the lodge at last took the opportunity of purchasing this property for £300. To do so it entered into a mortgage that was finally discharged only in 1950 for in the interim the members had had to expend further large sums in maintaining and improving the facilities. Indeed a sum of £400 was provided at the very outset just for interior decoration and to enable the merchant's warehouse, which lay alongside the entrance, to be converted into the temple which we largely see today. The hall has thus had a century of loving care and attention and its present condition fully reveals the devotion of present as well as past members. Amity being a lodge that meets every other Wednesday from October to March and once a month from April to September it can be appreciated that this is very much a masonic 'home' for its members and their guests.

To enter the house today is to be at once aware of the efforts made to retain something of the style and character of the original residence. Turn immediately left from the entrance hall and you will find yourself in what could still be a gracious dining room for the merchant and his family. The room runs the whole length of the four front windows and has a long mahogany table with matching high backed chairs, all provided by past brethren. The artefacts which are on display were gifts from previous members and the glass fronted cabinets at the end of the room reveal a selection of nineteenth century glass, a set of stamped rummers, items of silver ware, and a cribbage board for the use of otherwise unoccupied masons. Today this is but the robing room for the brethren and one can only marvel that they can gather in such a delightful setting.

Most striking in this robing room is the fireplace that once stood in the lodge room upstairs and which gave the only heating during meetings. It was designed to the requirements of a PM in 1874 and was made in a local pottery works. It is in terracotta and has a very distinctive design. Across the top of the fireplace run the words

LET BROTHERLY LOVE CONTINUE

and beneath this is a circle containing the signs of the Zodiac, with a Glory in the centre and also four phases of the sun. On the last part of this top panel are two scenes juxtaposed: the one showing an ear of corn near to a fall of water, and the other a winding staircase with an upreared dolphin having a square and compasses superimposed.

Down the two sidepanels of the fireplace we have, at the left, the second degree tools, with a figure beneath accompanying the words 'Lodge Amity 137' and then below this the first degree tools. On the right we see the third degree tools, another figure and the words 'Consecrated 1765' and at the foot of this section a circle with a triangle within it and a G at its heart.

The merchant house facade with lantern over door.

Behind this room we pass into what was originally the first section of the garden though that has now been built upon to form the elegant dining room. One is struck by the beautiful marquetry in the ceiling and the stamped leather medallions that adorn the walls and it is hard not to imagine that this was part of the original home. The effort to merge twentieth-century building with earlier construction is very evident. The carved wooden doors of this room and the carved oak fireplace and overmantel are also worth noting, together with six Georgian silver candlesticks and some pieces of the old glass that have been used constantly through the years. In glass fronted cabinets you will find a fragment of the old Grand Lodge banister which has been turned into a gavel, a different kind of French prisoner of war creation than those usually found around the country—the decoration for an old clock, as well as many other examples of masonic china, jewels, silverware and other smaller items connected with the history of Amity Lodge. There is also a fine carved oak sideboard on which stands the marble statue of the Earl of Zetland who presented the Centenary warrant in 1865. It is certainly one of the most attractive dining rooms in any masonic hall and it is naturally a matter for local pride.

Two flights of stairs lead to the rooms above. These consist of an elegant room behind the upstairs windows of the façade, a smaller robing room used by the Past Masters' and the temple itself. The effect of white panelled walls and fitted carpets on the stairs and in the two former of these rooms gives a sense of dignity and well-

The view from the Senior Warden's pedestal with the heavily carved panelling.

being. It also reflects that care that has been lavished on these premises by the past and present members.

In the longer room upstairs there is a picture of the older lodge room arrangement during the period 1880 to 1910, the first indication of the Newfoundland connection and a picture of the Lion & Lamb.

In the smaller of the rooms there are pictures of William Williams, a Provincial Grand Master, the Grand Master, Lord Blayney who signed Amity's warrant, RW Bro Lord Llewellyn, another PGM, a fine portrait of Thomas Dunckerley and a warrant written, sealed and signed by him and dated 1780 authorising the Poole brethren to hold a Royal Arch chapter. The most interesting item here, however, is an ancient masonic picture which demonstrates the pre-Union symbolisation, in human figures, of Faith, Hope and Charity. This picture lay discoloured and half-hidden until it was recently restored. The expense involved has been well employed for the picture is a unique memorial to an age of masonry that has passed.

It is time to enter the temple proper. As one would expect the room we are about to see is almost a living museum of masonic history—almost, because this is also a place where that Freemasonry which has been so actively pursued here through nearly $2\frac{1}{4}$ centuries is still vigorously and distinctively practiced in the midst of this collection of masonic archaeological pleasures.

The roof will quickly claim your attention. It is decorated in blue and gold with a large circle in the centre of the ceiling, with a Seal of Solomon (the interlaced triangles), enclosing a large G, within it. Its loftiness and simplicity gives a sense of space and ease to what might otherwise seem to be a floor space packed with objects. To add to the arrangement of the otherwise very plain walls there was provided in 1910 a set of 15 Spanish chestnut panels that were said to have come from a Spanish monastery of around 1500–1600 and may well have been part of the loot brought back from the Peninsular War by a member of the Wimborne family. The installing of these panels, which greatly enrich the appearance of the room, was paid for by Lady Wimborne of Canford Magna in memory of her husband. She is said to have paid £400 to the carpenter who took 12 months to set them in place. They were finally presented on her behalf.

To fit in with the original plan for the temple the members selected the present Wardens' chairs and their pedestals which thus add to the sense of overall unity but even the Master's Chair, which is Chippendale of unknown date and came from a non-masonic source, fits into the plan for in its decoration there is what looks very like a Sun in glory.

This is one of those lodge rooms in which in pre-Union times there was the older arrangement of two pedestals in the east. The fortunate visitor will be shown the original furniture normally in store. The one immediately in front of the WM is in fact an old prie-dieu with exquisite carving but there is no information about who produced this. The other pedestal once used, and of more simple form, has however a sun with its rays on the outer face and carries the 1810 Bible which has one of Thomas Dunckerley's plates in its inside cover. Mention of that remarkable mason is here fitting for on the wall of the lodge just inside the entrance you will see an original portrait of that peripatetic PGM.

Whilst speaking of pictures we shall later notice the portrait of a very special member of the Lodge of Amity (John Sydenham) who saved the lodge from

Another old working 'tile'.

An oil painting by an unknown artist depicting pre-Union symbolism. The figures of Faith, Hope and Charity are shown. The painting was discovered in the boiler room of Amity Lodge No 137 covered with dirt until recently restored. It is thought to have lain undistrubed since the 1880s.

extinction in 1830. The lodge itself did not meet for three years because there was division amongst the members over the issue of Parliamentary reform. During that time this worthy brother paid the lodge's dues to Grand Lodge in London and thus ensured not only that the Lodge could resume after its 'temporary setback' but could also claim 100 years of regular existence when the time of the Centenary occured. Elsewhere on the walls you will see the famous warrant granted to the lodge in 1765 by Lord Blayney, and we are told that the members elected to have the *coloured* version which cost three guineas.

On the north wall we come to the space that was once occupied by the terracotta fireplace seen now in the robing room below. Its replacement is a grand and substantial carved Victorian oak one and it has a mantelshelf that holds a great many objects of special masonic interest. They may indeed be regarded as the Lares and Penates of this ancient lodge. Here you will find other links with Newfoundland (for 9 members of Amity are members of lodges in that distant 'colony')—a piece of Labrador rock with its magical, blue fire texture, and a plaque depicting a map of Newfoundland and Labrador in a green mineral called Virginite which was a gift from the brethren there.

There is also a skull with a bullet hole over the left eye. It was for long buried and only recovered locally in the twentieth century. The theory is that Poole having been a Parliament stronghold, and nearby Wareham having been strongly Royalist, there was a skirmish in the environs of Poole and this was the skull of one of the unfortunate combatants. There is also a glass case containing the 'Amity biscuit' of 1833 but the interested visitor must learn that story of true masonic brotherhood for himself.

Another four items were obtained from Portsmouth by Thomas Mercer, a land waiter (or early customs officer), and five other merchants who gave £25 each to pay for their purchase. Of these we should notice the masonic charity box, which is an ex-tea caddy, that was to receive gifts from those who were unable to be present at the meeting. There is also the first ballot box of the lodge, called the Secretary's box and containing enough balls for each member to receive two. It is worth noting that the Treasurer here was once called the box-master, an expression that dates from the Regius Ms of 1390.

There are further gifts from overseas. There is a silver mounted Caribou horn which was sent by the District Grand Lodge of Newfoundland in 1979, whilst from Amity Dunedin in New Zealand there came a hardwood alms dish and a "feather box" made in that country from now extinct 'down under' birds!

This remarkable array of lodge specialities is completed with two other distinct items. One is the portrait made in 1860 of that Past Master, John Sydenham, of whom we have already heard whilst alongside him is the marble tracing board of 1780. It has features that immediately suggest comparison with what we have seen in Lewes and Taunton but there seems to be no idea of how this board came here. It remains a fascinating oddity.

Altogether this notable building is full of interest as, for example, with the organ used here which before its installation in 1933 had given great satisfaction to countless cinema audiences. From outside lantern to the interior 'bright morning star' one encounters everywhere the many pleasures contained in this meeting place. Visiting Poole is a must for any serious masonic student.

ST. AUSTELL

The Gem in the Capital of the Cornish Clay country

THE CHINA CLAY HILLS of mid-Cornwall are amongst the most distinctive and even weird features of this countryside or indeed of Britain as a whole and they tell the traveller that he is soon to arrive at the town of St Austell that nestles at the foot of the Carclaze Downs. The town itself has its share of good-looking buildings with the Georgian Quaker Meeting House from 1829, the Italianate Town Hall of 1844, and the eighteenth century White Hart Hotel. Holy Trinity Church has a fine perpendicular tower and some interesting carved figure-work in niches on the outside walls and good Early English style windows. Yet for the masonic visitor to this part of Britain there is another treat in store. As he climbs the approach to the centre called South Street he will be struck by a tall, gabled stone building which stands near the top on the right-hand side. It is the local Masonic Hall and it will well merit a pause by any visitor who can spare an hour or so.

Prior to the use of this, their own hall, the masons in Peace and Harmony Lodge No 496 (originally 728) used to meet in the White Hart Hotel mentioned already, and then later in the premises at Cross Lane. The lodge was actually consecrated in 16 July, 1844, the same year that the Town Hall was built and both events reveal how the town was growing in importance and wealth at the time. The first Worshipful Master, Bro Hodge, is still remembered by the photograph of him that is preserved in the present temple but his efforts and those of his contemporaries were not strong enough to prevent there being a lapse in the life of the lodge between 1849 and 1855 with the result that it was not until 1955 that the lodge could claim its Centenary warrant.

Once re-established the lodge found a new lease of life and so strong was its progress that by 1900 there was a successful move to their own premises on the present site. The cornerstones were laid on 20 June 1900 following a meeting in the Public Rooms of the town. From there the brethren formed a procession and marched to the new site headed by the Town Band. The chief cornerstone was laid by WBro Edmund Carlyon, who had already been a member of the lodge for 53 years, and who had therefore seen not only the resurgence of the lodge but could rejoice in its culmination with this ornate building. The other stones were laid by Bros Mason, Giles and Higman. The silver trowel used by Bro Higman at this ceremony was bought by the lodge from a descendant of his and is now on display in the temple, but sadly the one used by Bro Carlyon was sold when the local Penrice House and its contents were put up for auction and as the lodge members

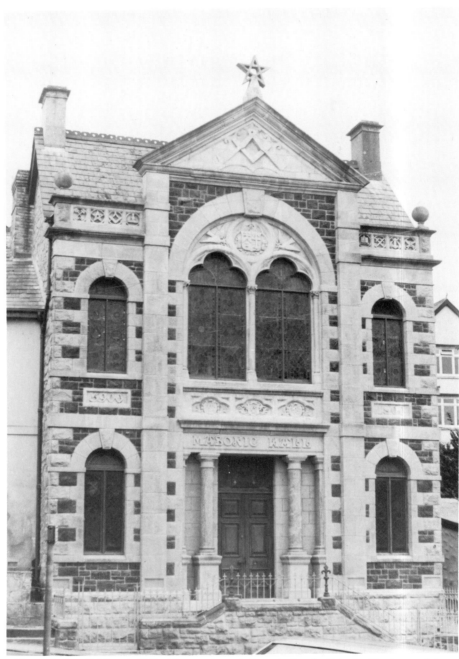

Above: *St Austell Masonic Hall with masonic symbols on the façade. Note the Keystone and doves.*
Right: *The windows of the temple.*

were unaware of the sale they could not go along and retrieve that one also. The cost of the whole project was £998.

Fortunately for the visitor today the full glory of the façade that must have emerged to the gaze of the first occupants is now restored and one can see the richness of the frontage which so properly reflects the similar wealth of detail within. The façade is a fine example of the ornate architecture of the time with some excellent mouldings and stone carvings—in their own way as memorable as those of the neighbouring parish church.

At the apex a pentagonal star surmounts the gable which has in its triangle a bold square and compasses in the Master's degree. This in turn surmounts an arch with a large keystone and the arch embraces two trefoil-headed windows of leaded lights with the coat of arms of the United Grand Lodge set in a circle between them and the keystone above. Beside the arms are two doves flying downwards with an olive branch in their mouths. On the balustrade which tops the front walls on either side of the arch are carved representations of the jewels belonging to the

The niche on the winding staircase with painted stonework.

principal officers of a lodge.

On the band of stone which extends either side from the heavy lintel below these upper windows are the two dates—5900_L^A and 1900_D^A—whilst the central portion below the windows has elaborate masonic symbols with the words MASONIC HALL inscribed below them.

The main doorway is a fine panelled one set between two elegant pillars raised on tall plinths and with severe but tasteful chapiters. A set of steps with rough ashlar facing and an iron railing across the whole leads up from the street whilst on the extreme sides of the façade at ground level there are two more lancet-style windows with stained glass and well-defined arch and keystone headings. The whole impression is one of immense care, great pride and harmonious workmanship. It is a façade to recall, and a fitting introduction to the interesting items within.

The ground floor area is occupied with a hall, refectory, kitchens and clothing room, and at the rear a fascinating winding staircase gently twists its way up to the temple above. On the way up one cannot but admire the niche set in mock stone paper, with a rounded half pillar on the base, carrying a bust in white set against a pale blue rear wall. The flooring here is yellow and black chequer and with the stone paper being extended above the stair there is a real sense of being in a small chamber. For the rest of the treads the wall decoration is mock-panelling so that one returns to a more intimate home-impression and in the dado of beige there are several masonic symbols on display. It is said that the original designers had no intention of making this staircase into a second degree feature but one cannot but think that someone had this in mind for it is done so well. It would have been so easy to create square corners.

At the top of the stairs one immediately encounters the beauty of the elegant and rich window designs that are lit from without. What may have seemed just dark window spaces from the street outside are now seen to be lesson aids in masonic symbolism. The style of the glass patterning is typically late Victorian but the colours are delicate and balanced and the circular roundels in each frame are full of all the implements that distinguish the officers of a lodge. With foliage and patterns of colour and other emblems all round the outside the effect is unforgettable and the visitor will have a sense of being in a cave of masonic mystery especially when he discovers the bookcase and its contents, the Masters' boards and the pictures that adorn this ante-room area. The loftiness of the ceiling, the delicate blue walls and the beige upper border all combine to calm those who gather here and not least those who are shortly to be candidates in the adjoining temple.

Through an adjoining door to the right you then enter the equally late Victorian lodge room used now by four Craft lodges, two Royal Arch chapters, one Mark and one Royal Ark Mariner lodge and one Rose Croix chapter. It is a room of which they are all doubtless very proud.

The main impression in entering the room is of overwhelming colour. For any who might be aware of the remaining medieval chapels in certain parts of Greece the effect is the same. Every part of the walls and ceiling is covered with shades of red, blue and cream. The rich blue carpet, with its quite small square of chequered flooring in the centre, the light blue ceiling between the rich brown and carved wooden beams, the red-curtained windows and the rich red boards of past Masters

The east of the temple with pentacle window and Victorian photographs on display. The walls are brightly coloured.

interspersed with a classically decorated blue dado—all these features create an amazing sense of solid stability and care. This is a room that was made to embody all the sense of pride and dignity and mystery that the craft of masonry is meant to engender. When the door closes you have a real experience of being in another world, looked down on by the four painted life-size figures of Justice, Prudence, Benevolence and Temperance as well as the hanging banners of the lodges that live here—and one, that of Peace and Harmony—being the original one of nearly 150 years ago. Here, as one commentator of Cornish halls has remarked, is a wealth of needlework quite apart from the other crafts displayed. The banner of the 1850s that shows two naked children playing happily with a recumbent lion is a masterpiece in itself for the quality of the original work shows through despite the passage of time and its ravages.

In front of the chequered square and at its west end stand two slender reddish wooden pillars with chapiters and two white globes above them, and with

Looking west with pillars and globes prominent. Of interest is the gong (left of picture) and the Inner Guard's chair. The 'G' is suspended from the ceiling.

rectangular plinths beneath. Between these two pillars and joining them is a cushioned kneeling stool about five feet wide and in front of each of the pillars are either a rough ashlar or the smooth one suspended in its tripod. In the centre of the square is a blue cushion with gold trimming, no doubt placed there to bear the working tools of the degree worked. Above this cushion hangs a gilded G from the ceiling.

The east end of the temple is quite distinct and attractive. It is raised on three steps to a dais with the Master's chair yet one more step above this. The chair, like those of the other principal officers, was made for the room when it was first opened and therefore fits naturally into the décor. This includes a series of wooden arcades with blue backgrounds and in every other arcade a golden square pointing downwards. In front of the red plush bench seating that runs along the whole east end there are similarly upholstered chairs for the IPM and Chaplain. Behind the Master's place is a most ornate stone feature that permits the display of some fine Victorian photographs including the first Master and other notables of the first generation. The feature is topped by a kind of crown and this, when the red curtain is withdrawn, fits well against the leaded light window that has in it a large stone pentacle. As one visitor has remarked: "It seems a strange thing that this window with its fine design is covered at lodge meetings and especially for Royal Arch ones!"

As one considers the detail not only of this centrepiece of the hall at St Austell but also in the rest of the building—the well-framed warrants, the attractive red-bosses in the dining room, the recently cleaned façade, the newly-arranged bar and the full-sized billiard table—one is left with the clear impression that this is still very much a masonic home for the many brethren who live in the locality. It is a hall that will continue to flourish in the second century of its life and will be remembered by many as a fine legacy of the last days of Victoria. It is certainly a gem to be discovered in one's travelling through the peninsula—and one not soon forgotten.

TAUNTON

A Tribute to Taunton's taste

EVEN DESPITE THE care and attention given in the present century to the property in the Crescent, Taunton, there yet breathes over the extended rows of brick-faced, white sash windows and basement-fenced houses a sense of eighteenth century affluence and solidity which nothing can destroy. It is within this area of an older Taunton town that there was built a Roman Catholic chapel which was at last acquired by the Taunton Masonic Hall Co Ltd in 1878. The company had been formed specifically for this purpose by members of Unanimity & Sincerity Lodge No 261, and it was made plain that shares in the property could only be held by 'members of the Order of Free and Accepted Masons'. From that date to the present the ownership of the hall has been vested in, or controlled by, members of that lodge.

Preceding 1906 a number of members of the lodge had transferred their shares to the lodge free of cost and the lodge itself had bought shares as funds allowed. In 1909 the Directors of the Company recommended that the lodge should be the sole owner and that the Company should be wound up. This action was agreed by the lodge members. Whilst ownership of the hall vests in elected Trustees on behalf of the lodge, the day to day management since 1938 has been in the hands of a Committee of representatives elected from all the lodges.

In 1919 the Trustees purchased the adjoining property, No 20, thus enabling the supper room to be enlarged and central heating to be installed. It was this latter step which explains why a visitor takes the apparently unusual step of bypassing the imposing neo-classical entrance to the hall, with its fine pair of pillars and the triangular pediment, and seeks entry by a smaller, if pleasant, fanlighted doorway to the left of the hall façade and through an entrance that suggests that it is another professional firm that one is wanting to visit. The firm indicated is actually a tenant of the Trustees, thus providing useful income for the proper maintenance of what is an imposing building. The whole complex now comprises a supper room, a sherry room, kitchen, cloakrooms and cellars as well as the main temple. During the last world war the supper room and No 20's accommodation was taken over by the American forces.

After passing through the simple but well-ordered entrance hall we move along to a narrow lobby which acts as a tyler's area before we pass into the main temple. The contrast on entering this principal room is very striking for we now perceive the interior of that fine colonnaded exterior at the corner of the terrace. The half columns which decorated the exterior are now seen to be projected into the temple and reach from floor to ceiling, pure white against the rich crimson wall-covering in between. There is an immediate sense of spaciousness and dignity enhanced by the magnificent arrangement behind and around the Master's chair.

The east end is composed of a white stone base in the form of a square alcove with solid projecting sides. It is capped with a gilt frieze and above this base at a height of 5 ft there rise on the projected arms two sets of double round columns with gilded chapiters carrying a pediment of classical design picked out in gold. Above the whole entablature are the customary words in gilt:

AUDI VIDE TACE

On the crimson wall behind the Master's chair and above the white base of the alcove are the framed warrants of the oldest lodges that meet here and above them the beautifully framed and preserved original banner of Unanimity & Sincerity Lodge. The present banner reveals the same features as its earliest precursor but the manner in which the older item is kept would be an object lesson to many brethren who are similarly privileged elsewhere to have a banner of equal antiquity. Such items need and justify proper preservation and display.

In front of the fine east end stands the three-stepped dais for the Master's chair and pedestals. I say *pedestals* advisedly because in addition to the taller white cubic pedestal, bearing a gilded square on its front panel, that stands immediately in front of the WM there is, on the first step of the dais, a smaller mahogany desk with inlay on its front panel (originally an old gramophone cabinet!), a plush kneeling pad and cushion. It is on this 'pedestal' that there lies the VSL and it is here that the candidate kneels to take his obligation.

Surrounding these two pedestals are three chairs for the WM, IPM and some distinguished Grand Officer, each of them highly individual and yet together creating another facet of this 'memorable' room. The present Master's chair was made by J. White of Taunton in 1807 (5 January) and has a tall, oblong, red leather back with a golden Glory etched into the centre. The chair's two upright supports are fluted wooden columns with decorated pediments carrying two miniature globes in tiny metal tripods. Between them there is a semicircular panel of wood at the heart of which is an open book with the square and compasses crossed upon it. Of especial delight and showing exquisite tooling is the panel that runs across the bottom of the seat's back beneath the leather panel. This openwork panel shows a trowel and a maul cut in precise detail, with a level dividing them and running flush with the leather seat, the whole encompassed by a semicircle of floral carving. The same care and detail is shown on a panel below the seat and below the carved front legs. This again displays four masonic symbols.

The IPMs chair would do honour to any WM throughout the land. It is entirely gilt, save for the ample crimson plush seat, the crimson centre of the gilt oval backpiece and the upper parts of the armrests. The legs are chamfered and taper from the base of the seat to the ground whilst the small gilt panels at the corners of the seats and at the foot of the recessed arms carry delicate representations of opened dividers. Rising from the cushioned seat at the rear of the chair the oval back is flanked by two perfect gilt pillars with square bases, fluted bodywork, flowered capitals and polished white balls at their head. To complete the elegance of this chair it carries at the top of the oval, gilt, framed back a gilt spray of acacia

Opposite: View of the east of the temple at Taunton.

The unusual warden's chairs with pillar backs and distinctive level and plumb rule emblems.

and an opened book bearing the square and compasses crossed. The chair was made in 1789 and purchased, like its neighbour, in 1807.

By comparison the other chair of the three main ones on the dais is rough and solid and suggests an ecclesiastical origin. Fashioned in almost jet black oak it is beautifully carved over its whole surface and with its ample crimson seat balances quite adequately the other partners in the east. It is in fact one of a set of three, the others being used by the Deacons. Though it bears a director of ceremonies symbol it was moved to the dais when it was replaced by the new DC's chair mentioned later. It is to be imagined that the loftness of the temple, the pillared east and the choice quality of the furniture all combine to impress those who come into this one time church.

Yet there are other distinctive features to which one's attention may be properly directed. Most prominent amongst these is the array of items that stand constantly on the west end of the chequered carpet during Craft ceremonies.

On the outside of this display stand two slender white pillars on square bases with curved chapiters and above them two globes set in semicircular metal frames. The pillars are some 12 feet high and reach to the level of the decorated gallery and organ loft that stretch across the whole west end of the temple. Between their fixed bases stretches a crimson kneeling bench, and immediately in front of this bench stand two more antique globes, the celestial and terrestrial, in oaken holders with tripod stands.

Between these globes is a most unusually formed tripod. The arms, unlike those normal elsewhere, are formed in a gentle curve to the apex and each of the ribs is carefully tooled and grooved. The whole effect is of added strength but there is little sense of it being an operative hoist. It is however a most delightful piece of speculative masonic furniture. It is matched by another such tripod to the south of the plinth stand, and between them they suspend the rough and smooth ashlars with miniature brass pulleys. Being painted on the first degree tracing board they are perhaps older than one might suspect.

We now encounter the centrepiece of this display—a light blue silk covered plinth that stretches some six feet or more down the length of the temple. At the centre of it is an ark of the covenant, a carved, gilded and flat-topped box, with rings in the sides for two gilded poles with which it is carried about. On the top of it stands the gilded pot of manna with imitation stalks in it, whilst around it are placed the various working tools of the three degrees. At the east end of the silken cover stands a large firing glass and a brass letter G.

Even more intriguing for the 'offcomer' (as non-locals are usually described) are the three items that stand on the carpet leaning against the east end of the plinth. These are, on the left, a black-framed pair of marble white tablets bearing the Latin numerals I to V, and VI to X (an obvious reference to the 10 commandments given to Moses—see also the Barnstaple hall in this volume): whilst on the right is something peculiar to Bridgwater and Taunton. It is variously described as 'Euclid', 'Proposition' and 'Alms' Board or the 'Drawing or True Tracing Board of the Master'. A little of the history of how the significance of this board was recovered will explain why there is an apparent mixture of names for it.

In June 1857 a Bro W. E. Bracey started to read through the minute books of Rural Philanthropic Lodge, No 291, Highbridge, which was warranted in 1793. He came across the term 'one board Euclid' and this led him to enquire whether others knew of a similar term. The Secretary of Perpetual Friendship Lodge, No 135, Bridgwater, warranted in 1764 sent him a picture of their 'Proposition' board which had been stored away but was now displayed in their lodge ceremonies. It then occurred to a PM of Unanimity & Sincerity Lodge that they had a similar board which was used as the 'Alms' board when addressing a candidate at the north east corner. (Here see the same kind of 'tile' used in the hall at Lewes in this volume).

This led to the present item in Taunton being freshly cleaned thus revealing many hitherto hidden details on it. When the Bridgwater and Taunton boards were compared alongside each other it was clear that though the former was in a better state of preservation it was identical in size and general layout and was a genuine part of a lodge's normal furniture when first devised. Both boards are of solid mahogany, about $\frac{5}{8}$ of an inch thick and 12 in square but with top and bottom projections where tools or drawings on the boards realistically protrude beyond the edge of the main surface. The main portions are painted in brown shades but the designs and scales are in black as are the surrounds.

The Taunton board was painted on a white lead priming and the crinkly marks have been caused by age, because the varnish had contracted. On the top of it are the words "The First Book" and underneath "Proposition XLVII" and then a

The floor display with curved tripod, large globes, ark, tile and the tablets.

diagram of it. The Ground Plan in the centre denotes that of King Solomon's Temple but the most prominent feature is a hand, with a cuff of the late eighteenth century, holding a pair of compasses. On the right of the hand the capitals of three Orders of Architecture are shown.

It would be impossible here to enter further into an analysis of these boards but it would seem that they were made towards the close of the eighteenth century and were used in both lodges for some years until the vogue of having a set of three tracing boards came in. In Taunton this was in 1808 whilst in Highbridge it was not until 1863. Certainly the presence of this item makes this hall and its furniture all the more memorable.

The third of this trio of special items is a heavy metal keystone with a cramp at its head. It is unusual in that the item is split into three moveable parts and it would seem to be what was originally known as the 'mark of Lewis'. Some may recall it having been worn as a cap badge at the Royal Masonic School for Boys.

Yet we cannot leave this temple without looking however briefly at various other distinctive items. The Wardens' pedestals probably date from 1817 and with their respective symbols in gilt on a white background complement the upper pedestal in the east. The Wardens' chairs are of a later date (1858) and were made by George S. Stevens in the town. Whilst in no way so ornate as the other principal chairs described already they are far from ordinary. The leather oblong backs are flanked by fluted pillar-style supports with plain wooden balls in carved holders at their head, a solid wooden triangular panel between them and attached to the rear of that panel but displayed above it a large wooden level for the SW and a plumbline for the JW. With tapered, grooved legs and a decorated seat base these chairs add their measure of dignity to the whole lodge layout.

In the centre of the north wall there stands the substantial chair of the Director of Ceremonies. This is not the only place where we have seen this distinctive placing of this important officer (See the hall at Bath in this volume) but in this case the chair that he occupies is much more prominent. Not only are the seat and back well padded in leather but the surround is gracefully carved, there is the D of C symbol on the headpiece and there is an ample platform for the officer to stand on when in position during the ceremonies.

Flanking the DCs chair are two curtained areas on the wall with a third further along at the north end of the dais. These curtains cover the lodge tracing boards which are now framed and mounted there so as to preserve them from the inevitable deterioration which would have ensued if they had not been cared for. These tracing boards, with their highly distinctive designs, are illustrated in the 'Freemasons Guide and Compendium' by Bernard E. Jones. They were originally painted as floor cloths in 1808 by Bro William Dight, a 'limner' who was initiated in the previous year. For many years they were used as such but because of wear and tear they were then enclosed in frames that took two stewards to move them. From 1956 it was felt right to remove them from the floor altogether to their present honoured position. The curtains are of course drawn back according to which ceremony is being worked.

As we proceed out of this fascinating room we shall notice the fine organ in the balcony at the west end. In its white wooden casing with the pipes in gilt and blue this gracious instrument was provided from the residue of the estate of WBro J. G. Vile and was placed in position in 1932. Its ample chords well fill this vast and lofty space. We cannot part from the Taunton hall without pausing for a moment in the 'Sherry room' which has received its name as a delightful social area before mounting the chequered carpet steps that lead to the adequate dining facilities in the rear of the building. In this elegant room, which has its own mosaic carpet, there is a well arranged collection of early jewels, warrants, old certificates, medals, aprons and lodge boards with the names of Past Masters. With its own portable organ in one corner the room has a facility as a LOI or to help in other degrees but together with the silver and plate that it also houses it is a treasure trove for the enquiring mason. The collection of items here was started in 1838 and the first masonic books were presented as long ago as 1842. Bro May who made that first gift wrote in his minute book that it was his hope that they would be 'a nucleus around which would be ultimately formed a library worthy of the lodge'. Whatever might have been his hope for the library his contemporaries must rest happily in the assurance that they have left to masonry universal a hall and its contents that many will continue to enjoy and appreciate.

The impressive entrance to what was once a Catholic Church.

TORBAY

The Masonic Hall at Torbay

IN THE COURSE of reading this and the companion volumes that describe memorable masonic halls in England we have time and time again been delightfully amazed at the remarkable scenes that await those who penetrate the premises used by the masons in this town, or that, and have had much occasion for thankfulness that local masons should have taken so much time and trouble to produce the beautiful settings in which to carry out our ceremonies. It is increasingly my conviction, after seeing so many such places around our country, that what must impress many candidates is not only the care and sincerity exercised by masons in carrying out our degrees, but the truly imposing or attractive surroundings in which they come to light and find themselves. It is not difficult to be proud of so many halls in which we meet.

The richly decorated temple at Torbay. The west wall is a remarkable painting with pillars and window effects as if looking at the setting sun over Paignton.

The hall at Courtland Road, Paignton, is just one. Its façade is not impressive, like others that we have seen, but once you have entered the double doors you are aware of the care and attention that have been taken by those who presently and in the past have occupied these rooms, to make them worthy of what is carried on there. In only three years time that occupation will have reached its first century.

The Torbay Lodge No 427 was formed a century before that in 1772 when George III was king. Paignton was then a town of 2000 people with streets that were irregular, narrow, dirty and ill-kept. The houses were similar having walls of mud and roofs of thatch and giving an overall mean appearance. The main public buildings were the parish church and a posting house called the Crown and Anchor Inn. It was in this hostelry that William of Orange sought lodging after his landing at Brixham in 1688 and it was also here that the Torbay Lodges, 427 and the present 1358, had their birthplace before the inn was demolished in 1892.

It was there, at a time when the population was growing through the families and dependants of the officers of the British fleet that was blockading France, when slavery was still permissible and press gangs roamed the neighbourhood, that Torbay lodge met in the upstairs room. It continued until 1824 when it was erased through 'want of members', even though the Worshipful Master and Senior Warden at the time were blood brothers. The incident that seemed to signal the lodge's serious state was on a cold autumn evening with the fire burning brightly in the large fireplace and the two brothers started an argument over ritual that eventually led to one of them, being full of the local strong ale, picking up all the aprons he could set his hands on and flinging them into the flames. In those days of local production of such items that gesture was itself a form of death blow.

The painted alcove ceiling above the master's chair.

The unusual warden's chair with the painting by A. G. Wallis behind.

For some 45 years there was no longer a Torbay lodge though the True Love and Unity Lodge No 248 had appeared in 1782, and the St John's Lodge was established at Torquay in 1810. By 1871, however, a brother, W. E. Warren, summoned a meeting at the Crown and Anchor again and it was there agreed that 'it is desirable that a Freemasons Lodge should be established in Paignton'. A warrant was granted on 26 May and the consecration was performed during a meeting of the Provincial Grand Lodge at the Old Town Hall on 3 August in the same year.

In 1890 a new site for the lodge premises was denoted by Bro Bridgeman. Specfications were prepared and tenders invited from lodge members. The tender of Bro Rabbich amounting to £663 was accepted and on 15 April 1891 the foundation stone was laid by WBro Bradford, the lodge secretary, and Bro Bridgeman. The completed premises were duly consecrated on 11 August. A new and striking internal decoration was carried out in 1930 and in 1985/6 all the lodge room décor was restored to its original colours by WBro Parsons.

It is to that inner sanctum of the dedicated premises that we should now take ourselves up the short winding staircase to the left of the main door and what we will find there will certainly impress with its detail and quality. In 1929/30 it was the work of WBro Arthur G. Wallis, who was well known in Paignton as an artist, and who undertook to give the temple its distinctive appearance. In his own words. 'To know the meaning of anything clearly in one's mind is a great help to the enjoyment of it' and he would have been the first to want those entering here to understand the designs and motifs that are so beautifully executed.

The division of the ceiling by cross beams into three distinct areas suggests that the sky, representing the vast extent of a masonic lodge 'in length between East and West, in breadth between North and South and as high as the heavens', is to be regarded as in separate parts. In the centre are the constellations as they appeared in the mid-night sky on the night that the lodge was consecrated—Ursa Major, or the Plough, appearing over the Secretary's desk and pointing to Polaris or the North Star. In the midst of these stars is the conventional 'G'.

To the east the scene is of a glorious dawning showing how the cloud formation appeared one day over Torbay in August 1929. It thus has particular appropriateness for this lodge. Whilst over the Junior Wardens' chair the arch and roof joinings have been most clearly disguised to show more clouds surrounding the sun at its meridian. This is very well achieved by cutting off the ceiling night sky by a wooden beam that is part of the hall's construction.

In the west and framing the charmingly simple and arched chair of the Senior Warden there is the scene of a setting sun whilst higher up on the wall and to the Senior Warden's right is a moon in its first quarter thus illustrating the words "the moon to govern the night . . . '. It is particularly as we look at the west end of the temple that we begin to realise how carefully the pillaring painted on the walls has been chosen so that the three orders of architecture, Doric, Ionic and Corinthian have been the designs chosen even though their placing has encountered certain problems.

The first idea was to have two pillars flanking each chair and the concept was realised in the south. Here the beams form a very satisfactory stop for the entablature and enable it to be used as a sort of frame for the scene above. In the case of the east and west ends the recessing in the wall would have cut off the Ionic

Looking east with the secretary's desk on the left. The master's chair is richly decorated and together with the painted pillar and arch effect on the walls makes Torbay one of the most colourful temples in England.

and Doric entablatures at just the point where they would be effective and so the solution adopted was to have a pair of columns on each side and thus create a colonnade effect. This arrangement is seen to perfection at the west end where the triglyphs, or grooved tablets, and the metopes, or square panels, appear with special grandeur. It is when you are gazing on this part of the temple that you need to realise that the whole surface of the walls are quite flat and that the only truly 3D items in the room are the wooden beams of the roof. The painting is so powerful and so well executed that you have the remarkable sense of standing in a much larger and more extensive area.

The arcading around the whole room is also most delicately presented and consists in the north of gentle arches resting on slender double pillars with descriptive decorations between each arch space and in the spandrels between each arch. In these latter spaces are the usual compasses, square, VSL, whilst scenes representing the passwords of the second and third degrees are represented in some of the arch decorations. These are surrounded by a Celtic type of interwoven tracery in light blue representing the unity of Freemasonry and the various spaces have the Craft, Mark, Royal Arch implements, as well as the various forms associated with the lodge officers, D.C., Chaplain, Steward, etc. Most attractively sited is the motif over the entrance, on the inside, where it reads,

Seek and ye shall find: Ask and ye shall have: Knock and it shall be opened.

These arches on the north wall are especially well arranged because the corbels supporting the roof timbers could not be avoided and they have been disguised by resting on the painted pillars beneath. Moreover, the space for the door has dictated the arrangement of the spaces here and thus six arches replace what was an original plan for four. The style is Romanesque because it has an historic connection with Freemasonry in that the sacking of Rome led to the spread of operative masons across Europe. What was not perhaps noticed earlier is now apparent — the figures in the spandrels are surrounded by the acacia, the pomegranate and the lily.

Detail of part of the wall decoration.

The amazing detail that is contained in the wall paintings is evident in these views.

The south wall, having windows, has arches with a single twisted design suggesting a more English appearance and indicating the more developed skill of masons as they crossed the continent. It is here, and because the flow is interrupted by curtains, that one notices the dark blue frieze that bears its own succession of masonic symbols. The colour of the background prepares the eye for its transition to the ceiling scene above whilst the various coloured figures displayed also connect one with the much more elaborate designs below.

One is thus led into an awareness of the gracious combination of items and effects that make this a most attractive place in which to gather. This is in no way disturbed by the properly more ornate treatment of the centrepiece at the east end of the room. The colonnade here is of black Ionic columns with white chapiters, the whole framing a similarly arched Master's chair but one of much more ample proportions, with a backrest of rich blue bearing a fine armorial crest that sits majestically above the pedestal when the occupant of the chair is absent. It is a piece of fine Victorian design and of Gothic form. Being placed amongst its pillars, that support a rich painted archway with its keystone, and an entablature bearing a radiant sun device, and above it a further sloping panel having the Seal of Solomon and a pentacle at its ends, the whole has an eastern Mediterranean appearance and something of what King Solomon's Temple may first have suggested. It should also be remarked that the pillars of the colonnade are so well painted that they give the right appearance wherever in the temple one may sit.

It would be wrong to merely dwell on these superbly renovated items of wall decoration even if they are the principal feature of this quite unexpected and remarkable temple. One should note that all the items of this room are clearly chosen and maintained with especial care. The pedestals are of excellent finish and have their emblems beautifully executed on their frontages. The desk of the Secretary is no less wonderfully finished with its brass and crimson angle lamp, whilst the floor covering would grace any temple anywhere. It covers the whole floor between seats and pedestals and has not only the usual chapter borders but a further rich golden fringe of other designs. The chairs for those sitting aflank the Worshipful Master and for the deacons are of no less quality than those of the principal officers whilst the subdued colour of the comfortable wall and bench seating for others fits perfectly into the whole colour scheme.

Here, then, is a room of real distinction. It may once have been a 'bleak and rather uninteresting room' when it was first taken over but there can be but little doubt that the masons of Torbay Lodge have every reason to regard their present home as one of the finer masonic dwellings in the country. With what pride they must look time and time again on that scene behind the Senior Warden's chair as they came to close their proceedings. They see there no less than the skyline of Paignton from the park or as near to the lodge building as any skyline could reasonably be seen. The Parish Church, St Joseph's Monastery and Primley Hill are all represented with the sun actually setting behind the church tower. Here, in their very midst, is the place to which they are to go out as brethren who have nothing to be ashamed of and much to be grateful for. They leave their abode of peace and rest with glad hearts and proud memories. Anyone who may have the delight of joining with them will, I am sure, have no less an experience of joy. Here is a hall that one leaves with regret but with happy remembrance.

WEYMOUTH

A Return to Regency Times

IT IS EASY BOTH to find this Hall and to remember the age in which it was built. As to its location you make for the promenade at Weymouth, look for the great statue of King George the Third, stand at its base with your back to the sea and look left up the main street of the town. One hundred yards down on the right hand side you cannot miss it. Its fine neo-classical façade stands out from the tall row of Georgian buildings that surround it. With its protective railings on a raised forecourt, the two great fluted pillars at the entrance supporting a frieze and triangular pediment, and the blue doorway surrounded by rusticated stonework with a keystone at the top of the arch it would hardly be more possible to draw attention to this meeting place.

As to the date of its foundation, the stone was laid in the same week as the Battle of Waterloo. The occasion was marked with much gaiety and the party that followed was, we are told, so rowdy that some of the brethren who attended were scandalised to the point of giving up Freemasonry altogether. The debris of the party was also so great that the tyler was paid a guinea to clear up!

Despite the impressive front of the hall the remainder is purely functional. Moving down the side of the building in School Street one sees the length of the temple interrupted by a blue side door which is the entrance for those attending lodge today. This is followed by the gabled end of the dining room and then a house which is the home of the resident tyler and caretaker. The whole complex is quite extensive and well maintained.

Entry by the blue side door leads you into a lobby corridor from which you first gain access on the left to the large dining room. One is immediately impressed by the fine fireplace made of Portland stone. In an entablature on the mantelpiece is the following inscription:

The Memorial Stone
to commemorate the prosperous state of
Freemasonry in this Town and Province
was laid this 15th Day of December 1876 A.L.5880,A.D.1876
in the 40th year of the reign of
Her Majesty Queen Victoria Patroness of the Order
H.R.H. Albert Edward Prince of Wales, K.G.R.W.GM
by R.W.Bro. W. Eliot, P.P.G.M. Dorset

On the headpiece immediately above the actual fireplace are the following names:

Pelly Hooper W.M.

H. T. George S.W.   C. R. Crickmay   T. A. Hanne J.W.
                                     Architect
                                J. T. Whettam-Builder

The William Eliot mentioned in the inscription was a banker from Dorchester who followed William Williams as Provincial Grand Master in 1839. His reign in the Province was brought to an untimely end when the bank with which he was associated got into difficulties in 1846 and he felt compelled to resign. His portrait adorns this room as do the smaller sized pictures of the Earl of Shaftesbury, William Tucker and William Williams who were also Pr. G. Masters. The fireplace would be enough to commemorate his rule in the county but there is also on the adjacent wall a glass-fronted box containing his collar as the Provincial Grand Master which is alongside a full length portrait in oils in which he is wearing the collar.

The floor display and Zodiac ceiling are prominent features at Weymouth.

The room contains many other fascinating pieces. There are shields that indicate the Hall's connection with the Order of the Knight Templar. In 1780 the first Grand Superintendent of Dorset was the ubiquitous Bro Thomas Dunckerley, who was not only Provincial Grand Master but also Grand Master of this new knightly order. Under him there was warranted one of the first Templar Encampments in the 1790s under the title of the 'Durnovarian' (Dorchester) and though its existence seems to have been a short duration ending in 1804 we still see here some of the shields belonging to that body. These underline the links in this building between eighteenth century and present day Freemasonry and this is further strengthened by the presence of shields from yet another, if early nineteenth century, creation, the All Souls Preceptory that functions to this day.

There is one of the not entirely unique 'skull' pictures which, when looked at with concentration and from a slightly different angle, turn out to be a scene showing two children sitting beneath an arch. It is still an intriguing *trompe l'oeil*. Another illustrated picture shows the famous 'Symbolic Mason' who is made up into something like a human figure by the arrangement of all the tools and implements used in our speculative ceremonies and rituals. Even though the picture is known elsewhere it again adds a feel of history and character to this meeting place. It is a sense of the past that is reflected in the large display cabinet to the right of the fireplace, where we find an imposing array of masonic pottery. Here can be found not only mugs and tureens, punchbowls and plates that once graced the dining tables, bearing their tell-tale lodge name and number, but even a large urinal pot that was passed around we are told, beneath the table. Nothing could more graphically remind the visitor of boisterous evenings and sumptuous tables after the lodge ceremonies upstairs that make any current ribaldry and noisy conversation pale into insignificance.

Still, as interestingly, the walls carry further reminders of the past. There is a framed box containing the supposed scarf and pipe used by the Duke of Sussex, famed leader of the Craft at the time of the union of the two eighteenth century Grand Lodges. There is a picture of the famous 'Harper' R. Arch jewels of which the Chapter has a full set and, more unusually, a set of jewels representing those worn in the breastplate of the High Priest in the Jewish Temple and collected for display here by the Rev Neville Hutchinson. A large coat of arms being those of the Antient Craft of Masons and Weymouth, on a shield of Portland Stone, carved and presented by John Selman, completes the array of wall decoration.

Yet most fascinating of all in the dining room is the famous '1571 Chair'. The origin, life and final presentation of this old and distinctive piece of furniture in which the WM sits at the festive board is a story in itself. It may be briefly told as follows.

On 12 September, 1895, a letter was sent from the Worshipful Master of the All Souls Lodge to the Mayor and Town Council of Weymouth. That letter contained the following passage:

> ... Amongst other items of interest (in Minutes belonging to the Masonic Order in Weymouth) I find that a lodge called "Arimathea" existed in this place ... from February, 1809, to March, 1828, and the members possessed an old Sixteenth Century Chair, which since 1828, or thereabouts, has been, first on the Weymouth side in the Town Hall, and then in the Hall on this side. The members of the 'Arimathea' Lodge, when their Lodge ceased working, joined

'All Souls' which was founded in 1767, and is still, as you are aware, working. Mr S. C. Weston, whose statue is in your Hall, gave a chair for 'All Souls' Master in 1821, and Mr W. Eliot gave the other large chair in February, 1828. I mention these two facts to show that the reason the chair now in your Hall was not taken direct to 'All Souls' Lodge' was that there was no proper place or room for it. . . . I think I am right in saying your Corporation has no use for this Masonic relic, and we shall be glad to have it restored to its proper use. If you think well, we would give you another chair for it, but in any case we shall be exceedingly obliged to you if you will return it to us, and thank you for having preserved it so long.

Yours faithfully,
J. Howard Bowen. W.M.170

In response to this letter the Corporation agreed to return the chair and the following account of its return is part of this Hall's history.

'AN INTERESTING CIVIC CEREMONY AT THE MASONIC LODGE'

On the evening of Monday, October 7th, 1895, the Mayor, Mr T. H. Williams, accompanied by the Town Clerk, Sir R. N. Howard, attended 'All Souls' Lodge in semi-civic state, for the purpose of formally handing over to the lodge the antient Masonic Chair which has, for many years, been in the custody of the municipal authority. The chair, which is a massive and magnificently preserved piece of furniture, has an interesting history. It was formally the Master's chair of the old 'Arimathea' Lodge ... It has been carefully preserved, and was recently restored at considerable cost. . . . Some difficulty

Weymouth Masonic Hall with its classical exterior.

The two Master's chairs. That on the right is used in the dining room whilst the chair on the left is used in the temple.

presented itself in regard to the ceremony (of handing it over), owing to the fact that the Mayor is not a member of the Craft, but (following a London precedent) the authorities were able to invite the Mayor to the Lodge in person, and to arrange a ceremony of a very interesting character. The Mayor arrived shortly after 7 o'clock, and entered the Lodge wearing his chain of office, accompanied by Sir R. N. Howard, the Town Clerk, who, though a leading member of the Craft and a Past Officer of the Grand Lodge of England, attended as a 'stranger'.

The Mayor and Town Clerk were conducted to the dais and the W.M. welcomed them in eloquent terms. He said . . . . . It was the first time they had been able to salute a Mayor of the Town who was not a Mason . . . and it might interest his Worship to know that Masonry appeared to agree well with the Mayors of town . . . because he found that during the last 95 years there had been 46 Mayors, and of these, 21 had been Masons. . . .

In reply the Mayor mentioned that though not a Freemason himself he had two sons who were members of the Craft, and a third would be made a Mason this week in London. He was, therefore, in a sense, connected with them, and he was proud of it. . . . He was delighted to attend that night for the purpose of returning the chair to its rightful owners . . . and as a memento of the occasion he had caused a silver plate to be placed on the chair, stating the circumstances of its restoration.

The mayor was then escorted round the lodge room and objects of historical interest were shewn to him. He was then escorted to the banqueting room where the ancient chair was to be occupied henceforth by the Master and, the lodge meanwhile being closed, he was joined by the brethren at a banquet. The usual loyal *and* Masonic toasts were honoured, and the healths of the WM, The Mayor and the Town Clerk were received with much enthusiasm.

It is worth adding that it was at this same lodge meeting that a VSL in large print was presented for the use of the Chaplains of the various degrees practised there.

The lodge room around which the Mayor was conducted during his visit had been but recently, in 1888, re-arranged and renovated. In this alteration the Lodge was sited due east and west, the present dais for the WM and Past Masters was

The west of the temple with painted shields prominent together with the unusual screen around the walls.

introduced, there was a general re-decoration and the construction of a kitchen 'with all the necessary appliances'. The dais, as a picture shows, was erected in an apse under an arch supported by Ionic columns with characteristic frieze, cornice and capitals, with the spandrels filled in and the mouldings ornamented with appropriate masonic designs, embracing pomegranates, lilies, wheat etc. all picked out in white and gold.

The Past Masters sit on a landing with five steps up from the floor with the W Master's chair up a further two steps and the back of the arch draped with a rich curtain in blue and gold. The walls were re-painted in vermilion and now carry a full length oil portrait, which is of that same Provincial Grand Master, William Williams, save that in this picture one sees the rich pomegranate at the join of the collar and apron and notes that, as was then customary for full dress regalia, the gloves were attached to the cuffs.

The chairs at the principal positions in this lodge room are of outstanding design. The Worshipful Master's chair is ample, with a tall back on which are designed the sun, moon and stars together with other devices and having two small celestial and terrestrial globes at the apex of the two pillared sides. This and the four flanking chairs with their carved devices for the IPM, Chaplain and two other

The dining room with engraved fireplace. The large portrait is of RW Bro William Eliot who was Provincial Grand Master of Dorset from 1839 to 1846.

PMs were all given by that same ex-Mayor of Weymouth, WBro Christopher Weston, and the WM's chair was once used in the Lodge of Friendship, No 61 in London. No pedestal stands immediately in front of the WM's chair but there is a small and tasteful case which holds three volumes—one each for 'Arts and Sciences', 'Statutes' and 'Masonic Laws'.

The pedestal used for obligations is, as now seen most usually in the USA where older practice has been retained, on the floor of the lodge at the east end of the lodge carpet. The cushion on its top is marked 'Arimathea Lo. 256' and the movable but permanently fixed square and compasses bear the date AM 5809, i.e. 1809 of the Common Era. To the right and left of this pedestal and at the end of the rows of seats for the brethren there are two very gracious globes set in cradles which are perched on slender, curved tripods. They show yet another arrangement for these regular features of an older masonic lodge and certainly add to the dignity and significance of the room.

On the north side of the temple are the two carved chairs for the Secretary and Treasurer, each bearing carved and guilded emblems of their offices—the two crossed quills and the upright key. Before their table and in the middle of the lodge stands the box for the tracing boards with three white candlesticks around it in the positions of the Master and his Wardens. The tracing boards were the gift of Bro T. H. Browne, Esq, Acting Master of All Souls 226 on the day of the Jubilee, 25 October 1809. The features of the first degree board that merit a special mention are a ladder that reflects the actual item being used in Amity Lodge, Poole—with its two sides encompassing a circle at the base and its rungs rising over a VSL open at the first chapter of St John's Gospel; a beehive; a pair of compasses open in the second degree position; three quite differently-sized columns showing Athene, for Wisdom, bearing a book and helmet on top of one, Hercules, for Strength, wearing eighteenth-century dress and having a club and pedestal one on top of another, and Venus, for Beauty, also in eighteenth-century clothing on top of the 3rd.

The second degree board is no less striking with its usual divided scene save that the Temple of Solomon appears at the top, shows a whole temple façade on the top of a mount, with a door half open in the 'middle' of the façade and the whole surmounted by three figures of the 2 kings and master workman (HA) around the central dome. The ascent to a forecourt painted like a mosaic pavement is by seven steps in a 90° curve and the whole is framed by two detached pillars with network hanging from the globes at their head. Below, in the lower half, is the Camp, allegorically that of the Israelites but in fact a representation of the camp occupied by those prisoners of war in Napoleonic times who were detained locally. The scene is outside Weymouth with the spires of Dorset in the distance.

The third degree board follows the same distinctive trend in that whilst it has a coffin with the usual sprig of acacia and the numbers 5:5:5 it also shows the lid slightly opened and within a shrouded body having a wound to its forehead. On the lid are also written

M.B.
T.B.C.
A.L. 5809
A.D. 1809

and the skull and crossbones below with a robed Aaron and his incense pot to the left of the coffin. Above the whole there is yet another scene, which might be thought to be Joppa but is something of the Dorset coastline.

Immediately above these distinctive boards in their case is the central ceiling decoration with its blue base, gold figures and gold rim showing at the actual centre a Seal of Solomon, surrounded by a blazing star and that still further surrounded by the signs of the Zodiac. Just to the north of this feature is a small golden circle surrounding a G and to the south a similar circle with the crossed square and compasses.

The west end of the temple is also packed with items of special interest. In the south west of the Temple stands a covered table bearing items of operative masonic meaning—a more than normal sized tripod with a pair of winch wheels to wind or lower the suspended ashlar; a rough and smooth ashlar, the latter with a clamp, and a keystone marked Y/9; a delicately-made Jacob's Ladder with the letters F, H and C upon it; a rule and a single column. For those in the Operative degrees of Freemasonry the association will be at once obvious.

Behind this table and stretching all round the west end of the room with two arched gaps for entry is a slender wooden screen which bears the chapter shields, and others that suggest the knightly orders mentioned earlier. Beneath an imposing western gothic style arch of this screen the Senior Warden's chair is raised up on five steps. Again there is no pedestal but rather a long table on the lodge floor carrying another tripod and suspended ashlar, the Poor Box given by Bro Arbuthnot in 1810, and another cushion for the apron of the appropriate degree being conferred. Looking up from this table you see the two great pillars of this lodge against the west wall, surmounted by two carved figures and above them, and all round the room just below the ceiling, larger knights' shields in full colour.

The whole effect is of a temple with great character and from an age that has passed, but is here happily retained. If as we descend once more to the street entrance and pause at the banqueting room laid ready for a dinner we would notice two last reminders of those Regency times. Before the 1571 Chair, and half way down the Senior and Junior Wardens sprigs, we would see three silver candelabra—the WM's holder having seven arms, the SW's having five and the JW's three. They were a gift to the lodge after having belonged to the Galway Militia XCI. Around them, and beneath their gentle light, you would see the generations of firing glass marks that still indent these tables.

WINDSOR

Within a Royal Borough

IT TAKES BUT a few moments for a walk of a few hundred yards straight out of the main gate of Windsor Castle to reach the Masonic Hall in Church Lane. In the midst of so many attractive and time-honoured buildings and streets, among them Charlotte Street—reputed to be the shortest street in England—the hall fits easily and fittingly, for it is very much an integral part of the borough's past. Dates for the hall's erection have been given as varied as 1705 and 1726 but any discrepancy here is easily explained. It was in 1705 that a resolution was made '. . . by the chief inhabitants (of the town) with whom ye Dean and Canons have likewise expressed their readiness concurr' to open a subscription list for the setting up of a Charity School. The purpose of this school was to be the education of '. . . the considerable number of children of the Town and Parish of New Windsor who have little or no education given them through ye povertie of their parents'.

The first name on the subscription list reads, 'Our Gracious Sovereign and Queen Ann' and she donated a sum of £50. There follows a list of the nobility, clergy and citizens of Windsor who subscribed varying amounts, including £10 from the 'Mayor and Bailiffs'. A much larger bequest '. . . to buy or build a house for the School' amounted to £500, and formed part of the will of one Theodore Randue (1642–1723). He was at some time Keeper of Windsor Castle and was also a most generous benefactor to other objects in the Borough.

A considerable period passed between the opening of the subscription list and the actual building of the school premises. (This delay was undoubtedly due to the fact that the bequest of £500 mentioned above was tied up in a will and did not therefore become available for use until after the death of Theodore Randue in 1723.) The earliest document of the Windsor Castle deed box is an exceedingly interesting one, namely, a Grant or Faculty making a gift of a narrow strip of land in the north-east corner of the churchyard which was to be added to that already available to the school builders. The deed is dated 23 March 1724 and the land measured 38 ft by 4 ft. This document at least suggests that no building took place before 1724 and thus brings us to an erection date like the second one mentioned above—1726.

A copy exists of the actual summary of the cost of putting up the building (£510 0s 8d, including a fair sum for legal fees) and this reveals that there would appear to have been a building of some sort on the land previously, as some un-named gentleman was paid the magnificent sum of £3 1s 0d for 'pulling down the old house and setting up the fence'.

It is often stated that the building was designed by Sir Christopher Wren but there is no documentary evidence to support this claim, and as he died in 1723 it is

The 'old school' door now with lantern and pediment.

hardly likely. It is true that he lived for many years in Windsor and was very much involved in the construction of the very gracious Guildhall completed in 1702. (It is worth inserting here that the present occupants of the Windsor Masonic Hall also use the Guildhall for their Installation meetings when numbers are too great for their limited premises around the corner). To revert to Wren, however, it seems that he may have been asked to comment sometime on what kind of building ought to house the new school and the result of the work done would not, I think, have been altogether unpleasing to him.

It seems that the present building served as a school from 1726 until 1862. The Royal Free School then moved to Bachelor's Acre, and the disused premises in Church Lane were sold to the then Castle Lodge No 1073—later to become Windsor Castle Lodge No 771—for the sum of £500. Considerable alterations were carried out to convert the school building into the beautiful temple and robing room that now exist and the members donated £708 8s 3d to cover the cost of the work involved. Unlike many of today's masonic centres, the Windsor Castle Lodge retains to this day the ownership of the freehold, although some eighteen other lodges and chapters enjoy the use of the building as tenants. At last on November 17, 1864 the ceremony of consecration took place and was followed by a banquet at the Guildhall for some 80 freemasons, with a bill for £26 6s 0d.

In addition to being the centre of Freemasonry in this royal borough the building has been put to other uses. As early as 1870 it is recorded that the robing room was let to the Vicar for a confirmation class of lady pupils. Opening the large black door which leads out onto the narrow strip taken from the churchyard one can see why the clergy would regard this hall as a useful adjunct to their premises.

The practical outcome of such an alignment was shown in 1907 when an agreement between the hall and the church allowed the electric power already connected to the Masonic Hall since 1902 to be transferred by cable to the church buildings. The masons can hardly be said to have profitted much from this gesture of help as their rent for the convenience was only 1/- per year! It is good to know that relations between the Parish Church and the brethren here are still warm and close.

During the 1920s and 1930s a Miss Ada Akery regularly held her ballet classes in the same room downstairs and to this day one of the sockets placed round the wall to hold the balancing bars for these would-be ballerinas catches the attention and curiosity of visitors as it is shown in the robing room display case. Between 1884 and 1909 this was also the headquarters of the local Infantry Volunteers— forerunners of the Territorial Army—and the building was licensed for the storage of their gunpowder!

Entering from the street through the canopied doorway one enters what at first appearance seems to be a normal domestic hallway. In a sense this is hardly surprising for on the left of the hallway is a door which leads into the living quarters of the hall's caretaker. The present occupant is a lady who exercises a motherly interest in the ancient premises and keeps the whole suite of masonic rooms in pristine condition. Recognising that the caretaker's dwelling extends from the doorway to the corner of the building at the top of Church Lane explains why, on the inside, this masonic hall is not quite so capacious as it might at first appear. It is not, however, its size that we are to admire.

On the wall past the caretaker's private door is an imposing "Astragal" fronted bookcase of three sections. It is marked 'The Library' and it is certainly well-stocked and seems to be much used. Next to that, but on the wall facing the front door, are a number of masonic portraits, including a fine one of the Revd Dr John T. Desaguliers, but also a most unusual piece—the Kirkwall Scroll. This coloured print, about 2 ft long and some 6 in wide, has its masonic-related contents fully explained in a framed panel alongside. Its contents are too long to explain here but any brother who reads it may truly be said to have made his one day's advancement in masonic knowledge. Alongside this there is also a 1794 Royal Arch certificate.

We now turn through the door on this same wall into the robing room. At once we are aware of the historic nature of this, the original schoolroom. The modest dimensions of the room, the presence of two fireplaces—one at either end, four cloth-covered tables, on the walls the rows of photographs of PMs of Windsor Castle Lodge and the masonic mementoes in a glass-fronted case, together with the several eighteenth century small paned windows, all combine to make this a fitting prelude to the still more intriguing rooms that await us above. One is here already aware of the school background to the building and can still imagine the classes that must have been held in groups around their respective tutors.

Beyond the windows at the rear one can, as already hinted, see the parish church of Windsor with its churchyard and on opening the solid wooden door at the rear one sees the small pathway, with its own gate to the street which was the result of the grant mentioned earlier. It runs the whole length of the hall, thus providing a welcome space for a smoke or for taking the air on the occasional warm evening when the lodge meets. Had this strip not been made available the hall would have no breathing space around it whatsoever.

Before passing upstairs mention must be made of the range of items contained in the display case in this room. Here you will find several Castle Lodge 'thistle-type' firing glasses, one large rummer and one silver tankard bearing masonic symbols. There are 4 decorated mugs about 6 in in height bearing two suns apiece (with faces and rays), as well as a circular band enclosing two pillars with globes, set on a chequered pavement, with a Glory and G at its centre between them. Above the circle is a fresh ear of corn. These charming mugs are joined by another large dish of china or porcelain most fully ornamented with masonic symbols.

Other more unusual items include a masonic $\frac{1}{2}$d in a glass cover and marked as 'available at the Black Horse, Tower Hill, Windsor'. There is a piece of wood marked as being a 'Portion of the beam at the Old White Hart where Shakespeare wrote "The Merry Wives of Windsor" . . .', a pair of scissor-snuffers, and a circular stone dish of three rings with one of the often encountered French prisoner of war jewels at its centre. Several bottles containing the corn seeds used at the consecration of local lodges provide a link with the past that is not too often seen.

Moving along a corridor from the hallway we come to a graceful winding staircase that leads into a compact ante-room in the shape of an L. On the left wall between two upper rear windows is a pleasant piece of marquetry in the form of a tray. It was presented by WBro F. Tress Barry, MP, PM of No 2 and No 4, a Past Grand Steward of England, in 1894. Its imagery is selective and apparently unconnected but it covers the Ich Dien sign of the Prince of Wales, the rose, thistle and daffodil, a mechanical crane lowering a stone on top of another beside an unfinished wall, a consecration table with two flagons against a pillared wall, two floating globes and a triangle containing the Windsor Castle motif above a square containing the Magen David

Looking east with chapter keystone alcove behind the pedestal and the large all-seeing eye above.

with a square and compasses at its centre. It is a very attractive item. Over the door into the adjoining temple are a pair of crossed tyler's swords.

From here we pass straight into the main temple. It clearly stretches the whole length of the hall and thus provides a vista worthy of the impressive wood panelling that covers the whole of the walls. The design of this most unexpected but tasteful room is thought to have been based upon the original temple in Great Queen Street in London before the days of the Million Pound Memorial building with which so many are familiar today. The impressive alcove arrangement at the east end is said to be especially reminiscent of the previous London arrangement and those who know the blue and gilt Master and Wardens' chairs kept in the Grand Lodge museum will now see how they must have looked.

The red plush chair here fits into a shallow rounded apse which tapers overhead to a strong semicircular gilded arch which has a prominent keystone bearing the Templum Hierusolymae sign. Flanking this arch are two columns with square bases, rounded stems and flowered chapiters. Across their heads and resting upon the top of the arch is a heavy architrave with moulded grooves and higher still, and above that, at the centre, is a most impressive golden eye, with golden rays bursting out from it in all directions. What is remarkable is that despite the overall richness and grandeur of this whole feature it is designed in the dimension fitting to this comparatively modest room and hence fits neatly into place. It certainly fixes the visitor's attention but it does not make the room seem top heavy.

In front of the widespreading Master's chair, with its elegant Regency style legs and accompanying footstool, there stands a no less attractive pedestal. This belongs to the Etonian Lodge of St John, No 209 which has met here since 1874 and is a most beautiful item of furniture. It is made of mahogany and bears upon its outer face another eye surrounded by a glory which perfectly balances the same feature above. Above this metal panel is another brass plate which carries the following notice:

> 'H.R.H. the Prince of Wales, K.G., M.W.G.M.
> obligated his eldest son, H.R.H. the Duke
> of Clarence and Avondale, K.G. as P.G.M.
> of Berkshire on this Pedestal at Reading
> December 15th 1890 who thereupon obligated
> W.Bro. T. Morland as Deputy P.G.M.'

That this event started a precedent is then marked by the fact that all down the sides of this pedestal one sees other smaller brass plaques which tell of the Duke's successors being obligated on this very pedestal but not always in Windsor. Thus the pedestal travels to where the new PGM is to be installed and thus forms a living link with his predecessors.

The origin of the pedestal itself is revealed in yet another plate's contents at the foot of the outer face. Here we read:

> 'This Pedestal was presented to the
> Etonian Lodge 359 (Later renumbered 209) held at
> Swann Inn
> Windsor in the County of Berkshire
> on the 7th day of December in the
> year of Masonry 5827 by . . . .'

and the names of the WM, JW and two Past Masters are then inscribed.

This, however, is not the end of the pedestal's features for inlaid on this face and between the gilded eye and the presentation plate is a most tasteful representation of a level with its loose string, encompassed by a set square and a pair of compasses. The whole piece is topped with a red velvet cushion on which lies the VSL belonging to whatever lodge is using the temple at the time.

The candleholders at the three principal officers' places are fine pieces of workmanship. These are the property of the Etonian Lodge and came originally from the well-known 'Vicar of Bray' Church. Also very striking are the SW and JW's columns which are made of polished brass and carry delightfully detailed globes at their head. These, together with the sparkling brass spirals of the SW's tripod and winch, complete the balance that again might be out-weighed by the impressiveness of the furnishings in the east.

The Warden's seats are not separate pieces of furniture here but are part of the permanent seating, in the form of forty-two knights' stalls, which occupy all the walls of the temple save for the northwest corner. Here there is an alcove for the organ. Extending now to three or four rows, above each stall are recorded the names of the Past Masters of Windsor Castle Lodge, dating back to the very first one in 1859. A picture downstairs of the lodge in 1905 reveals that there were then places on the walls where names did not appear. Those spaces are now all occupied.

The greatest surprise and peculiarity of this old temple comes whenever a third degree ceremony is due to be performed. Next to the Secretary's seat, marked with a pair of quills painted on to the rear of his stall, and with what appears to be a tall, old style clerk's desk before it—actually a baize-covered box cunningly devised to hide a very heavy marble altar—is a seat which can be removed. This gives access to a secret panel of door height which then allows the brethren to pass through into a smaller though quite complete lodge room, decorated throughout and carpeted in black! It has three charming, carved high-backed chairs for the Master and Wardens, three black, cubed pedestals with the sign in white for each officer, and a heavy maul upon the WM's pedestal, together with another older VSL which this time bears the inscription 'Castle Lodge'. Over the WM's place is a lamp, covered in black, but with an orange transparency which lights up to show 'that bright morning star'. It is a room with heavily-shuttered windows into which no natural light normally ever penetrates.

On reflection one realises that this dark room is but the extension of the space occupied by the anteroom at the head of the stairs, and explains why the main temple seems to be so much narrower on entry than would normally be expected from a space that lay over the spacious robing room below. Used for the Master Mason's degree it will be easily realised how useful a facility this dark room is whilst those who know other masonic ceremonies can imagine how they too can be well served in a place that was originally intended to be only a Craft and Chapter temple. The starkness of this inner chamber is very striking as well as unexpected and its presence in this old hall marks Windsor out as one hall that certainly needs to be specially remembered.

Retracing our steps through the main temple and out through its door we should notice one final item. Alongside the grille that permits a small part of the door panel to be opened from within there are three more brass tablets fixed to the door itself. They describe with affection three previous tylers of Castle Lodge. They were

Charles Nowell, who died in office at the age of 79, and served for 38 years;
Charles Mulford, who retired at the age of 86, and also served 38 years;
Jack Greenwood, who died in office at the age of 93, and had served 22 years.

It is the devotion and dedication of such men that has helped to make this hall, and its lodge, what we still see today. In honouring this hall we honour them.

The old school room, now a robing room and museum.

INDEX

People and Places

Objects and Symbols

The Halls covered in other volumes in this series are:

The MIDLANDS

Birmingham
Boston
Colchester
Ipswich
King's Lynn
Knutsford
Leicester
LetchworthLudlow
Norwich
Nottingham
Peterborough
Shrewsbury
Spilsby
Stamford
Stony Stratford
Warwick
Worksop
Great Yarmouth

The NORTH

Alnwick
Barton-upon-Humber
Berwick
Beverley
Bolton
Bradford
Carlisle
Durham
Huddersfield
Kingston-on-Hull
Liverpool
Manchester
Newcastle upon Tyne
Sunderland
Wakefield
Warrington
Whitby
Whitehaven
York
Halifax